Out of the Ordinary

Recipes From
The Hingham Historical Society
Hingham, Massachusetts

This cookbook is a collection of favorite recipes,
which are not necessarily original recipes.

Out of the Ordinary®
Recipes From
The Hingham Historical Society
Hingham, Massachusetts

Published by
Hingham Historical Society

Copyright© 1998 by
Hingham Historical Society
P.O. Box 434
Hingham, Massachusetts 02043

Cover Photograph: Phil Swanson
Illustrations: Barbara Menzies

Library of Congress Number: 98-070445
ISBN: 9661892-0-5

Edited, Designed and Manufactured by
Favorite Recipes® Press
an imprint of

FRP™

P.O. Box 305142
Nashville, Tennessee 37230
1-800-358-0560

Book Design: David Malone
Art Director: Steve Newman
Project Manager: Jane Hinshaw

Manufactured in the United States of America
First Printing: 1998   6,000 copies

Foreword

Hingham, Massachusetts, took its name in 1635 from a community in Norfolk County, England, and was incorporated as the twelfth town in the Massachusetts Bay Colony. Hingham residents have always sought to preserve their town's historic past and maintain its beauty, and the Hingham Historic Society, founded in 1914, is proud of its part in contributing to the rich educational and cultural life of the community.

The society maintains the Old Ordinary, a unique house museum chronicling 350 years of Hingham life and history, and the Old Derby Academy building, home of the original Derby School, now an elegantly restored facility serving as the Society's headquarters.

Each spring, the Hingham Historical Society sponsors one of the oldest house tours in the country. Since 1924, visitors have been welcomed into many of Hingham's most elegant and historic homes. Numerous programs are offered for the membership and townspeople, as well as for children attending schools in Hingham. Special exhibits, events, and lectures are regularly scheduled, and members are encouraged to participate in every aspect of this all-volunteer organization. Of notable interest are annual history and art awards for students and awards presented to homeowners and businesses for special achievement in preservation and restoration of historic buildings.

The cookbook is one more opportunity to preserve Hingham's heritage by recording the food and drink of Hingham's best cooks. We hope you will enjoy it.

Eugene R. Chamberlain

Eugene R. Chamberlain, President
Hingham Historical Society

Contents

Acknowledgements

Although many friends have shared in the compilation of this book, there are some who have worked especially hard and made outstanding contributions, which we would like to acknowledge.

We are very grateful to Barbara Menzies for her lovely illustrations, which have enhanced this book. Phil Swanson, as always, produced just the right photographs for our cover.

Rus and Lorena Hart's gracious introduction links our past to our present, while Cynthia Wilkins and Winston Hall provided interesting information about Hingham's many landmarks.

We thank Tony and Joy Greedy of Hingham, England, Rose Kocar of Hingham, Montana, and Joyce Kuhlow of Hingham, Wisconsin, for their perseverance and enthusiasm in pursuing recipes from their own Hinghams.

Our friends at Bowl and Board were generous with their time and expertise and we are grateful for their assistance.

We give special thanks to Talbots for their generous contribution. The history of this outstanding firm is an important part of Hingham history as well.

We owe a debt of gratitude to the Hingham Historical Society Board of Directors and their President, Eugene R. Chamberlain, for their confidence and support in making this book possible.

Finally, we would like to recognize Julie Lyons for her contribution, which was clearly above and beyond the call of duty.

Hingham, Massachusetts, has amassed a rich historical record and, consequently, conflicting tales and myths abound. We are well aware that this book does not contain every story and tradition that our readers could wish. We hope you will enjoy the ones we have included.

The Hingham Historical Society Cookbook Committee

Susan Achille

Virginia K. Bartlett, Co-Chair

Treena Crochet

Ruth Diezemann

Jeanne Hirsch, Co-Chair

Julie Lyons

Eileen Macedo

Sunny MacMillan

Barbara Menzies

Nancy Reid

Gloria Trowbridge

The Buttonwood Tree

Hingham's Buttonwood Tree is approximately 63 inches in diameter,
16½ feet in circumference, and 90 feet tall. One story suggests that it was planted by
Hosea Sprague, who lived from 1779 until 1843. As he explained, "The Buttonwood
that I set out fifty years ago in 1793 in front of my father's house has the appearance
of age. It is 30 inches in diameter 1 foot from the ground and is 75 feet high."
He would have been 15 years old when he says he planted the tree. Hosea's father,
Isaac, was the grandfather of another and more famous Isaac Sprague,
who was an artist, botanist, and friend of artist and naturalist John James Audubon.

Introduction

A cookbook is not just a manual of recipes. It is also a historical
record of food. How appropriate, then, that this one should come
out of the Old Ordinary, in past centuries a wayside eating place
for travelers, in a town which has recorded its history since the days of
the first town clerk. Appropriate, too, is the inclusion of recipes
from much older Hingham, England, and much younger Hinghams in
Montana and Wisconsin. The book, like our town in Massachusetts,
is a rich stockpot of old and young.

Our Hingham has lived through many changes. The 17th-
century Puritan village grew into the 18th-century town of traders,
shipbuilders, and farmers, whose spacious square houses still line our streets,
shaded now by Victorian trees. The industrial hustle of the 19th century
faded, and the shrinking town became a summer resort. Newcomers—first
Irish, then Nova Scotians, Dutch, and Italian—added their spice to the
mixture. Following World War I, affluent suburbanites chose
Hingham as a pastoral retreat.

During World War II, with its naval shipyard and ammunition annex,
Hingham became a military depot. In the post-war
suburban explosion, it burst at the seams with new young families, and its
ancient town-meeting character appeared doomed. Alarmed conservationists
mobilized to save a heritage of colonial homes and open green spaces.

Through all this change, those ancient activities—the
production and preparation of food—endured. First settlers on their
home lots fed themselves with their vegetables, chickens, pigs, a milk cow,
and apple trees. Grain, flax, orchards, sheep, and cattle filled
the 18th-century landscape.

In the early 1880s, trading ships transported salt mackerel and crops. The ships, crops, and barrels were Hingham-made. So were the famous buckets, the Howard ploughs for tilling, and Stevenson's scales and balances for weighing.

After the Civil War, locally grown fruits and vegetables, livestock, homemade jams, butter, and cheese were displayed at annual agricultural fairs. Henneries, piggeries, dairies, and market gardens survived the suburban assault of the early 1900s. The land values became so high that a retired farm manager told us a decade ago, "I don't believe there's a cow left in Hingham now." The grain mill of the 1640s and the millpond have long since been sepulchered under a parking lot. The last roadside market has closed.

So we return full circle to the home plot, the homegrown, the homemade. Many of us have adult children who call for remembered favorite entrées, breads, cookies, and pies. The want the record, the recipe. What is more deep in the human psyche than the memory of food, engaging all the senses? The editors of this book, honoring this truth, have blended history and memory with the preparation of food.

Lorena Laing Hart

Lorena Laing Hart

Francis Russell Hart

Francis Russell Hart

The Sister Hinghams

⟨E⟩ Hingham, England

Between 1630 and 1643, it is estimated that 20,000 people of all ages and from all walks of life left England in search of a new life in the New World. Among them were nearly 200 inhabitants of the small town of Hingham in Norfolk, England.

Families made the risky journey for many reasons: economic problems at home, the hope of free land, a spirit of adventure, and the desire for religious freedom. They left an ancient village that had probably been a Saxon settlement, but the origin of its name is lost in antiquity. The *Domesday Book* gives the town several names, among them Hingham Regis, indicating that Hingham once belonged to the crown.

In the early nineteenth century, Hingham was a bustling market town, and the population grew to almost 1700 residents. The advent of the railroad in neighboring towns, however, and the general decline of market towns contributed to a loss of population. In recent years there has been some revival in the growth of the town with new housing and small industry, and the present population is just under 2000.

The village of Hingham, England, is a living museum, with numerous 16th-, 17th-, and 18th-century homes and buildings lining the narrow streets. St. Andrew's church, one of the largest and most impressive in the county of Norfolk, dates from the early 14th century. It is also noteworthy in that Abraham Lincoln's ancestor, Samuel Lincoln, was baptized here in 1622.

  ⟨E⟩   indicates recipes from Hingham, England
  ⟨W⟩   indicates recipes from Hingham, Wisconsin
  ⟨M⟩   indicates recipes from Hingham, Montana
    indicates prize-winning cookie recipes

W   *Hingham, Wisconsin*

Located near Sheboygan and Lake Michigan, Hingham, Wisconsin, was founded in the first half of the 19th century by pioneers from New York, Massachusetts, Vermont, and Maine and was named after Hingham, Massachusetts. Vast virgin timber forests covered the area, and Indians were a common sight around the village. Pioneers cleared the land for their farms; a log schoolhouse was constructed, and a teacher hired. Religious services were held in the school until after the Civil War, when the first church was built. Farming, sheep raising, dairy farming, and many thriving businesses supported the town in its earliest days. There were high hopes that the new railroad to the West would bring prosperity to the area, but scandal and corruption interfered, and Hingham was bypassed as a railroad center. Today the small village has a population of just under 500.

M   *Hingham, Montana*

Although there is no proof, Hingham, Montana, probably received its name from James Hill, the Great Northern Railroad tycoon. His goal was to give towns on the hi-line, as the area in north-central Montana is called, names that would be attractive to prospective residents. Homesteaders from the East filed a claim and agreed to live on the land for five years in order to claim it, starting about 1910. In 1911, there were already several businesses in Hingham, including stores, hotels and cafes, a bank, a newspaper, real estate and insurance firms, a blacksmith shop, an auto garage, and two saloons. During the drought years, many farmers were forced to leave, and eventually, the advent of supermarkets and the automobile caused many businesses to close. Early settlers included mostly Germans, Czechoslovakians, and Norwegians, and their descendants make up most of today's population of about 200.

CHAPTER ONE

In The Beginning

Appetizers — Beverages — Soups — Salads

Old Ordinary Kitchen

The kitchen of the Old Ordinary conjures up visions of blazing fires on snowy winter days, when stagecoach travelers were assured of finding a warm welcome in the historic inn. It was built circa 1680 as a "one-room" house with a ground floor, one room above, and an attic; additions were made in 1740 and 1760.

"Ordinaries," where an ordinary meal of the day could be purchased at a fixed price, were encouraged by the legislature to aid travelers. Several owners were tavern keepers, beginning in 1702 when Joseph Andrews, Jr., received a license "to sell strong waters—provided he send his customers home at reasonable hours with ability to keep their legs."

The Old Ordinary, listed on the National Register of Historic Places, was given to the Hingham Historical Society in 1822 by Dr. and Mrs. Wilmon Brewer. With recent exhibition rooms, it is now a 14-room house museum containing an extensive collection of period furniture, export porcelain, paintings, textiles, tools, and artifacts of Hingham history. The garden, with a design attributed to Frederick Law Olmstead, Jr., is cared for by the Garden Club of Hingham.

Baked Bean Soup

Ye Hingham Cook Book - 1901

Two cups of cold baked beans, two cups of tomato, five cups of water, two slices of onion, three stalks of celery. Cook together for forty minutes. Put through a sieve, season with two tablespoons Chili sauce, add salt and pepper to taste, and thicken with two tablespoons of flour in three tablespoons of melted butter.

Grandma Rising's Pea Soup

Sampler of Recipes - 1971

1 ham bone with meat	6 potatoes, medium size
1 lb package dried peas	1 medium onion, chopped
2 stalks celery, chopped	2 carrots, chopped

Cook ham bone and peas in kettle with water to cover. Add celery and onion. Cook slowly for 1/2 hours, stirring often. When peas are done, remove ham bone. Take meat off. Cut in small pieces and return to pot. Add cut up potatoes and carrots. Cook until soft. Add milk and water, half and half, if too thick. Serves 6 to 8.

ℳ Tortilla Pinwheels

1 pound ground beef
1 envelope taco seasoning mix
1 cup sour cream
8 ounces cream cheese, softened
4 ounces black olives, chopped

1 cup shredded Cheddar cheese
1/2 cup chopped onion
garlic powder and salt to taste
5 (10-inch) flour tortillas

Brown the ground beef in a skillet, stirring until crumbly; drain well. Stir in the taco seasoning and cook using the package directions. Set aside to cool. Mix the sour cream, cream cheese, olives, Cheddar cheese, onion, garlic powder and salt in a bowl. Stir in the ground beef. Spread the mixture on the tortillas and roll up. Chill, covered with plastic wrap, for several hours. Unwrap and cut into 1/2-inch slices. Serve with taco sauce for dipping. Yields 6 servings.

ℳ Sweet-and-Sour Chicken Wings

2 pounds chicken wings
garlic salt and pepper to taste
1 egg, beaten
cornstarch
vegetable oil

1/2 cup sugar
1/2 cup vinegar
3 tablespoons catsup
1 tablespoon soy sauce
1/4 cup chicken stock or water

Season the chicken with garlic salt and pepper. Dip into the egg and coat with cornstarch. Fry in oil in a skillet until brown; drain well. Remove to a baking pan. Mix the sugar, vinegar, catsup, soy sauce and chicken stock in a bowl. Pour over the chicken. Bake at 350 degrees for 30 minutes or until cooked through, turning after 10 minutes. You may substitute other chicken pieces for the wings. Yields 8 servings.

Horseradish Cheese Ball

16 ounces cream cheese, softened
1 tablespoon prepared horseradish
1/4 cup chopped green
bell pepper

1/4 cup chopped onion
1/2 tablespoon seasoned salt
1 cup dried chipped beef
3/4 cup chopped parsley

Beat the cream cheese in a mixer bowl until smooth. Beat in the horseradish, green pepper, onion and seasoned salt. Add the dried beef and mix well. Shape into a ball. Chill, wrapped in plastic wrap, until firm. Roll the cheese ball in the parsley. Chill, covered, until serving time. Yields 12 servings.

India Spread

8 ounces cream cheese, softened
1/2 cup crumbled bleu cheese
1/4 cup finely chopped dates

1 tablespoon lemon juice
1/4 cup chutney
3/4 cup chopped pecans

Mix the cream cheese, bleu cheese, dates, lemon juice and chutney in a bowl. Stir in the pecans. Serve in a hollowed-out fresh pineapple. Serve with crackers. Yields 6 servings.

Boursin

2 cloves of garlic, finely chopped
1/2 teaspoon kosher salt or
table salt
8 ounces whipped unsalted
butter, softened
16 ounces cream cheese, softened
1 teaspoon dried oregano, or
1 tablespoon fresh
1/4 teaspoon dried thyme, or
3/4 teaspoon fresh

1/4 teaspoon dried dill, or
3/4 teaspoon fresh
1/4 teaspoon dried marjoram, or
3/4 teaspoon fresh
1/4 teaspoon dried basil, or
3/4 teaspoon fresh
1/4 teaspoon freshly ground
pepper

Mash the garlic with the salt. Cream the butter and cream cheese
in a mixer bowl until light and fluffy. Add the garlic mixture,
oregano, thyme, dill, marjoram, basil and pepper and mix well.
Freezes well. Yields 15 to 20 servings.

Perfect Pineapple Dip

1 pineapple
8 ounces cream cheese, softened
1/2 cup chutney
1/2 cup sour cream

1/2 teaspoon dry mustard
1 teaspoon curry powder
sliced almonds

Split the pineapple into halves lengthwise, leaving the fronds intact.
Cut out the fruit in small chunks and set aside to drain, reserving the pineapple
shells. Mix the cream cheese, chutney, sour cream, mustard and curry powder in
a bowl. Spoon into the reserved pineapple shells. Sprinkle with almonds.
Spear the pineapple chunks with wooden picks for dipping. The cream
cheese mixture may be prepared ahead and refrigerated
until needed. Yields 6 servings.

Dilled Dip Mix

½ cup dried dill
½ cup minced dried onion
⅓ cup dried parsley
¼ cup dried basil
¼ cup dried tarragon

2 tablespoons garlic powder
1 tablespoon pepper
1 teaspoon grated dried
 lemon peel

Combine the dill, onion, parsley, basil, tarragon, garlic powder, pepper
and lemon peel in an airtight jar and shake to mix well.
Use the mix in dips, dressings, soups or stews, sprinkled over bread,
sprinkled over chicken before baking or added to bread dough or omelets.

For Dilled Dip, combine 1½ tablespoons of the dill mix with 1 cup nonfat
yogurt and ½ cup nonfat mayonnaise in a bowl and mix well;
chill, covered, for 2 hours. Yields 8 servings.

For Dilled Dressing, combine 1½ teaspoons of
the dill mix with ¾ cup mayonnaise and ½ cup milk in a bowl and
mix well; chill, covered, for 2 hours. Yields 8 servings.

Christmas in Merry Old England

*Each Christmas the Hingham Society erects a Christmas tree
with fairy lights in Market Place, or uses the chestnut tree growing
there. At five o'clock on the Saturday afternoon before Christmas, a hundred
or more people, carrying lighted candles in jam jars, gather for a
Carol Concert. After the service, the ladies provide hot mince pies
and mulled wine made from the traditional recipe on page 19.*

Mulled Wine

Grated peel and juice of
1 orange
½ nutmeg, grated
3 to 4 tablespoons brown sugar
1 cup hot water

1 cinnamon stick
4 whole cloves
½ to 3 ounces brandy (optional)
1 bottle inexpensive red wine

Combine the orange peel, orange juice, nutmeg, brown sugar, hot water, cinnamon stick and cloves in a large saucepan. Simmer for 15 to 20 minutes or until heated through. Add the brandy and wine. Simmer until reheated; do not boil. Serve hot. Yields 4 to 6 servings.

Mulled Berry Cider

8 whole black peppercorns
6 whole allspice
6 whole cloves

2 (3-inch) cinnamon sticks
4 quarts apple cider
2 quarts cranberry juice

Tie the spices together in a cheesecloth pouch, leaving a length of string long enough to hang over the side of a stockpot. Combine the cider and cranberry juice in a large stockpot. Hang the cheesecloth pouch over the side of the stockpot so that the spices are submerged in liquid. Bring to a boil gradually; reduce the heat. Simmer, partially covered, until the cider is heated through and the flavors have blended. Discard the spices. Ladle into cups or mugs. The cider may be lightly spiked. Yields 24 cups.

Grandpa Bottum's New Year's Punch

5 pounds loaf sugar

2 quarts water

juice of 6 lemons

grated peel of 1 lemon

juice of 6 oranges

5 whole cloves

2 blades of mace

2 cups green tea

2 cups brandy

4 cups Jamaican rum

4 cups Champagne

¾ cup Chartreuse

Combine the sugar, water, lemon juice, lemon peel, orange juice, cloves and mace in a large saucepan. Simmer for 10 minutes, stirring to dissolve the sugar. Let cool. Mix the tea, brandy, rum, Champagne and Chartreuse in a punch bowl. Sweeten to taste with the sugar mixture. Garnish with orange and lemon slices. Store remaining sugar mixture in a bottle. Yields 15 to 18 servings.

—From *Sampler of Recipes*, 1971

How Sweet It Is

Loaf sugar is simply refined crystallized sugar that has been moistened and pressed into hard cones called loaves. Traditionally, pieces were broken off or grated for use at the table.

Colonial Wassail Bowl

1 cup sugar   4 cups red wine
½ cup water   2 cups cranberry juice
3 slices lemon   2 cups strained lemon juice
2 cinnamon sticks   brandy (optional)

Combine the sugar, water, lemon slices and cinnamon sticks in a saucepan. Bring to a boil, stirring to dissolve the sugar. Boil gently for 5 minutes. Strain through a sieve. Combine the sugar mixture, wine, cranberry juice, lemon juice and brandy in a saucepan. Heat just until hot; do not boil. Ladle into cups. Garnish each serving with a cinnamon stick. Yields 18 servings.

Be in Good Health

That is the original meaning of the Norse toast from which the word "wassail" comes, and to drink the wassail was to drink to one's health and prosperity. During colonial times, wassail of spiced ales or liquors was drunk at Christmas celebrations.

Chilled Cucumber Bisque

¼ onion, finely chopped
1 tablespoon butter
1 tablespoon flour
3½ cups chicken broth
3 large cucumbers, peeled,
  seeded, chopped

1½ cups plain yogurt
2 small cucumbers, peeled,
  chopped (optional)
¼ cup finely chopped dill
  (optional)
salt and pepper to taste

Sauté the onion in the butter in a medium saucepan until translucent. Stir in the flour and cook for several minutes. Add the chicken broth and 3 cucumbers. Bring to a boil and reduce the heat. Simmer for 45 minutes. Let cool. Process in a blender until smooth. Chill until serving time. Stir in the yogurt, 2 cucumbers and dill just before serving. Season with salt and pepper. Yields 8 servings.

Chilled Red Pepper Soup

3 large red bell peppers
1 medium onion, chopped
  or sliced

1 clove of garlic, minced
2 tablespoons butter
4 cups beef broth

Grill the red peppers until blackened on all sides, adding hickory or mesquite chips to the briquettes to enhance the natural flavor of the peppers if desired. Place the peppers in a paper bag and let stand until the skin has loosened. Peel the peppers and remove the seeds, reserving all juices. Sauté the onion and garlic in the butter in a saucepan over medium heat until the onion is translucent. Add the beef broth and reserved pepper juices. Simmer for 5 minutes, stirring occasionally. Combine equal amounts of the pepper pulp and onion mixture in a blender container or food processor container and process until smooth and all ingredients are puréed. Chill overnight in a sealed container. Ladle into bowls. Garnish servings with a dollop of sour cream and cilantro leaves. Serve with Tabasco sauce, crushed red pepper and salt and black pepper to taste. Yields 4 to 6 servings.

Carrot and Squash Soup

1 clove of garlic, minced
2 shallots, minced
2 tablespoons vegetable oil
2 tablespoons butter
1 tablespoon chopped
crystallized ginger
1/8 teaspoon turmeric
1/8 teaspoon cumin

1/8 teaspoon cinnamon
1/8 teaspoon saffron
8 carrots, sliced
3 cups cubed peeled
butternut squash
5 cups water or chicken broth
1/2 cup cider
1 cup half-and-half (optional)

Sauté the garlic and shallots in the oil and butter in a large saucepan. Add the ginger, turmeric, cumin, cinnamon and saffron and mix well. Cook for 2 minutes. Add the carrots and squash. Cook for 4 minutes. Add the water and cider and mix well. Cook until the carrots and squash are tender. Process the mixture in a food processor or blender until smooth. Stir in the half-and-half. Yields 6 to 8 servings.

Old Ordinary Garden

It is believed that the garden of the Old Ordinary was designed by Frederick Law Olmstead as a wedding present to the Reverend and Mrs. Louis C. Cornish. Reverend Cornish was minister of Old Ship Church from 1900 to 1915. "Mrs. Cornish planted her garden with many old time flowers to preserve the colonial traditions of the venerable homestead," according to an eyewitness account in 1911. Currently the Garden Club, which is responsible for the maintenance of the garden, is involved in an ambitious naturalizing project for the woodland area surrounding the original Olmstead design. Rhododendrons, crab apple trees, azaleas, and English roses have been planted as part of an ongoing effort of enhancement and maintenance. The huge tulip tree in front of the Old Ordinary was planted about 1863 and for many years has sheltered the house and grounds.

Corn Chowder

5 large red potatoes,
peeled, diced

4 cups fresh or frozen
corn kernels

8 slices bacon, finely chopped

1 large onion, chopped

2 tablespoons butter, softened

2 cups fresh or canned
chicken stock

2 tablespoons flour

1 teaspoon salt

1 teaspoon pepper

2 cups light cream or
whipping cream

Cook the potatoes in water to cover in a saucepan until tender; drain
and set aside. Purée 1½ cups of the corn in a blender or food
processor; set aside. Cook the bacon in a large saucepan until crisp.
Remove the bacon and set aside to drain, reserving the drippings. Sauté
the onion in the bacon drippings in the saucepan until tender. Add the
puréed corn, bacon, potatoes and chicken stock and mix well. Blend
2 tablespoons butter and flour into a smooth paste in a small
bowl. Add to the chowder and mix well. Simmer until the chowder thickens,
stirring occasionally; do not boil. Season with the salt and pepper. Stir in the
remaining corn and cream. Simmer until heated through; do not boil.
Ladle into bowls. Top each serving with a pat of butter
and chopped parsley. Yields 4 servings.

Thick Lentil Soup

1 cup dried lentils	4 large onions, finely chopped
4 cups water	1/4 cup chopped fresh parsley
1 tablespoon salt	2 fresh or canned tomatoes,
1/2 teaspoon dried marjoram	coarsely chopped
1/2 teaspoon dried thyme	2 tablespoons dry sherry
1/4 cup olive oil or vegetable oil	1/4 to 3/4 cup shredded Swiss or
4 carrots, peeled, cut into	Gruyère cheese
1/4-inch cubes	

Rinse and sort the lentils in a colander under cold running water.
Combine with 4 cups water in a 4-quart Dutch oven or kettle. Let stand,
covered, at room temperature for 1 hour. Add the salt, marjoram
and thyme. Bring to a boil over high heat. Simmer, covered, over low heat
for 1 hour; watch carefully to avoid boil-over. Heat the olive oil
in a large skillet over medium-high heat. Add the carrots and onions.
Cook for 10 minutes or until the vegetables are tender but
not brown, stirring frequently with a wooden spoon. Add the carrot
mixture, parsley, tomatoes and sherry to the lentils and mix well.
Simmer, covered, for 1 hour or until the lentils are tender and most
of the liquid is absorbed. Pour the soup into a heated tureen.
Sprinkle with the cheese. May sprinkle the cheese into serving bowls
and ladle the soup over the cheese if preferred. Yields 10 servings.

Hungarian Mushroom Soup

1 large onion, chopped

5 cloves of garlic, thinly sliced

2 tablespoons olive oil

2 tablespoons butter

14 ounces sliced mushrooms

1/4 teaspoon cayenne

2 teaspoons dillweed

1 tablespoon soy sauce

2 tablespoons paprika

1/2 to 1 teaspoon salt

1 teaspoon basil

2 cups vegetable stock or chicken stock

2 tablespoons butter

3 tablespoons flour

1 cup light cream

1/2 cup sour cream

1 tablespoon lemon juice

Sauté the onion and garlic in the olive oil and 2 tablespoons butter in a large skillet. Continue sautéing while adding the mushrooms, cayenne, dillweed, soy sauce, paprika, salt and basil. Add the vegetable stock. Simmer, covered, for 15 minutes. Melt 2 tablespoons butter in a large saucepan. Whisk in the flour. Cook until brown, whisking constantly. Add the cream. Cook over low heat for 10 minutes or until thickened, stirring frequently. Add the mushroom mixture to the flour mixture. Simmer, covered, for 10 to 15 minutes or until heated through. Remove from the heat and let cool. Reheat before serving. Stir in the sour cream and lemon juice just before serving. Yields 4 servings.

Zucchini and Brown Rice Soup

1 pound zucchini

8 ounces spinach leaves

6 cups (or more) chicken broth

½ cup long grain brown rice

1½ cups sliced onions

3 tablespoons butter

salt and freshly ground pepper
to taste

Rinse, peel and grate the zucchini. Rinse the spinach leaves and pat dry; cut into thin strips. Bring the chicken broth to a boil in a large saucepan. Stir in the rice; reduce the heat. Simmer, covered, for 40 minutes or until the rice is tender. Sauté the onions in the butter in a large sauté pan until wilted and golden brown. Stir in the zucchini. Cook for 4 to 5 minutes, stirring constantly. Stir in the spinach. Cook just until the spinach wilts, stirring constantly. Stir the zucchini mixture into the rice. Season with salt and pepper. Cook until heated through. Thin with additional chicken broth if the soup is too thick. Yields 8 to 12 servings.

Corn and Scallop Chowder

1 pound bay scallops or
chopped sea scallops

2 (10-ounce) cans corn chowder

1 chowder can milk

¼ cup chopped red bell pepper

Cook the scallops in water to cover in a saucepan for 3 to 4 minutes; drain, reserving the cooking liquid. Place the corn chowder in a 2-quart saucepan. Add the milk, 1 chowder can of the reserved cooking liquid, scallops and bell pepper; mix well. Bring just to the simmering point, stirring constantly; do not boil. Garnish servings with chopped parsley. Yields 6 servings.

Old-Fashioned New England Fish Chowder

3½ to 4 pounds haddock
4 ounces salt pork, cut into strips
2 large onions, chopped

3 cups cubed potatoes
1 to 2 quarts milk
1 (12-ounce) can evaporated milk

Combine the fish with water to cover in a saucepan. Cook until the fish falls from the bones. Strain the fish stock; reserve the fish and stock, discarding the bones. Fry the salt pork in a large saucepan until crisp. Discard the salt pork, reserving the drippings. Fry the onions in the drippings in the saucepan until tender. Add the potatoes and enough reserved fish stock to cover. Cook until the potatoes are tender. Add the milk, evaporated milk and fish. Simmer until heated through; do not boil. This chowder is even better the second day. Yields 4 to 6 servings.

Hingham Fish Chowder

2 pounds any fresh or frozen white fish
4 potatoes, peeled, chopped
3 onions, chopped
celery leaves to taste
1 bay leaf
2½ teaspoons salt
pepper to taste

4 whole cloves
¼ teaspoon dillweed
½ cup margarine
½ cup dry vermouth
2 cups boiling water
2 cups whipping cream or evaporated milk

Combine the fish, potatoes, onions, celery leaves, bay leaf, salt, pepper, cloves, dillweed, margarine, vermouth and boiling water in a large casserole. Bake at 350 degrees for 1 hour or until the potatoes and onions are tender. Remove and discard the bay leaf. Stir in the cream just before serving. This can be prepared in a slow cooker, adding the cream just before serving. Yields 6 to 8 servings.

Salmon and Corn Chowder

3 slices bacon
1 medium onion, coarsely
  chopped
2 cloves of garlic,
  minced or crushed
2 tablespoons flour
2½ cups chicken broth
1 pound unpeeled red potatoes,
  cut into ½-inch cubes

1 medium green bell pepper,
  chopped
2 cups frozen corn
¼ teaspoon pepper
1 (8-ounce) salmon fillet, cut
  into ½-inch pieces
1 cup milk
¼ cup packed finely chopped
  fresh dill, or 2 teaspoons dried

Cut the bacon crosswise into ½-inch pieces. Cook in a medium saucepan over medium heat for 10 minutes or until crisp, stirring frequently; drain, reserving 1 tablespoon of the drippings. Stir-fry the onion and garlic in the reserved drippings over medium-high heat for 5 minutes or until the onion begins to brown. Stir in the flour. Cook for 10 seconds or until the flour is absorbed, stirring constantly. Add the chicken broth and potatoes. Bring to a boil over medium-high heat, stirring constantly; reduce the heat to medium-low. Simmer, covered, for 15 minutes or until the potatoes are tender. Return to a boil over medium-high heat. Add the green pepper, corn and pepper. Cook for 5 minutes or until the green pepper is tender-crisp. Purée half the chowder in a food processor. Return the puréed chowder to the saucepan. Return to a boil. Add the salmon and milk. Cook for 5 minutes or until the chowder is heated through and the fish flakes easily. Stir in the dill. Ladle into bowls and top with the bacon. Yields 4 servings.

Broccoli Salad

12 ounces broccoli florets, chopped

1 cup chopped celery

2 tablespoons chopped red or white onion

½ cup golden raisins

1 cup sliced water chestnuts, cut into halves

½ cup mayonnaise

¼ cup sugar

1½ tablespoons cider vinegar

Mix the broccoli, celery, onion, raisins and water chestnuts in a bowl. Combine the mayonnaise, sugar and vinegar in an airtight jar and mix well. Serve immediately or store, covered, in the refrigerator for up to 2 days. Add sliced mushrooms if desired. Yields 4 servings.

Broccoli and Bacon Salad with Walnuts

¾ cup mayonnaise

¼ cup sugar

2 tablespoons cider vinegar

8 slices bacon, crisp-fried, crumbled

4 cups chopped broccoli florets

½ sweet onion, chopped

chopped walnuts to taste

pine nuts to taste

Mix the mayonnaise, sugar and vinegar in a bowl. Add the bacon, broccoli and onion. Add the walnuts and pine nuts and mix well. Chill, covered, until serving time. Yields 4 to 6 servings.

Cranberry Broccoli Salad

1/4 cup sugar
1 1/4 cups chopped fresh
    cranberries
florets of 1 bunch broccoli
4 cups shredded cabbage
1 cup chopped walnuts

1/2 cup raisins
1 small onion, minced
8 slices bacon, crisp-cooked,
    crumbled
Mayonnaise Vinaigrette

Sprinkle the sugar over the cranberries in a small bowl. Let stand while preparing the salad, stirring several times. Mix the broccoli, cabbage, walnuts, raisins, onion and bacon in a large bowl. Add the cranberries. Pour Mayonnaise Vinaigrette over the salad and toss to mix. Chill, covered tightly with plastic wrap, for up to 24 hours. Toss before serving. Yields 4 to 6 servings.

~Mayonnaise Vinaigrette~

1 cup mayonnaise
1/4 cup sugar

1 tablespoon vinegar

Combine the mayonnaise, sugar and vinegar in a jar with an airtight lid; cover and mix well.

Cabbage Crunch Salad

¼ cup sugar	¼ cup margarine
¼ cup vinegar	8 ounces chopped almonds
2 tablespoons soy sauce	½ cup sunflower seed kernels
½ cup vegetable oil	¼ cup sesame seeds
2 packages chicken-flavor ramen noodles	1 medium head cabbage, shredded

Combine the sugar, vinegar, soy sauce and oil in a saucepan and mix well. Bring to a boil, stirring occasionally. Let stand until cool. Chill in the refrigerator. Crush the ramen noodles. Reserve 1 flavor packet for the salad; set aside the second for another use. Melt the margarine in a large skillet. Add the noodles. Sauté until light brown. Add the almonds, sunflower seeds, sesame seeds and contents of the reserved flavor packet. Add the cabbage and mix lightly. Combine the dressing and salad in a large salad bowl and toss to mix. Chill, covered, for 1 hour before serving. Yields 6 to 8 servings.

Warning

She may dress in silk, she may dress in satin,
She may know the languages, Greek and Latin.
May know fine art, may love and sigh,
But she is no good if she can't make pie.

—From a Boston cookbook, 1926

Spiced Carrots

1 pound small carrots,
scraped, julienned
½ cup sugar
½ cup water
½ cup white vinegar

1 tablespoon mustard seeds
4 or 5 whole cloves
1 (3-inch) cinnamon stick,
broken into pieces

Blanch the carrots in boiling water in a saucepan for 3 minutes.
Drain and rinse the carrots under cold water; drain again. Place in a
large bowl. Combine the sugar, water, vinegar, mustard seeds,
cloves and cinnamon pieces in a saucepan. Bring to a boil; reduce the
heat. Simmer for 10 minutes. Pour over the carrots and let
stand until cool. Chill, covered, for 8 hours to 1 week. This may also
be served as an hors d'oeuvre or with a sandwich.
Yields 4 to 6 servings.

Perfect Potato Salad

2 teaspoons sugar
2 teaspoons vinegar
5 cups sliced cooked potatoes
1 cup chopped onion
1 tablespoon salt

1 tablespoon celery seeds
1½ cups mayonnaise
4 hard-cooked eggs, sliced
lettuce leaves

Sprinkle the sugar and vinegar over the potatoes in a large bowl.
Add the onion, salt, celery seeds and mayonnaise and toss to mix. Fold
in the eggs carefully. Chill, covered, until serving time.
Spoon into a lettuce-lined bowl. Garnish with parsley, sliced
radishes and/or additional slices of hard-cooked egg. Yields 8 servings.

Rice Salad

3 cups water
1 bay leaf
1 teaspoon salt
1 pinch saffron
1/2 cup uncooked converted rice
1/4 cup olive oil
2 to 3 tablespoons wine vinegar
or white balsamic vinegar
freshly ground pepper to taste
1/2 cup finely chopped seeded
tomato

2/3 cup finely chopped red onion
1/2 cup finely chopped celery
1/2 cup finely chopped red or
green bell pepper
1/4 cup raisins or currants
1/2 cup pine nuts, pecans or
walnuts
1/3 cup chopped parsley
sliced hard-cooked eggs
sliced tomatoes

Bring the water to a boil in a saucepan. Add the bay leaf, salt
and saffron. Stir in the rice gradually, maintaining the
water at a boil. Reduce the heat to low. Simmer, covered, for 11 to
15 minutes or until the rice is tender. Toss with a fork; drain.
Add the olive oil, vinegar and pepper and mix with a fork. Cook
until heated through. Add the chopped tomato, onion, celery, red
pepper, raisins, pine nuts and parsley and toss well, adding additional
olive oil or vinegar if needed. Spoon into a salad bowl.
Chill until serving time. Garnish with hard-cooked eggs
and sliced tomatoes. Yields 4 to 6 servings.

Tomato Aspic

2 (3-ounce) packages
lemon gelatin

1½ cups boiling water

1 (15-ounce) can tomato sauce

3 tablespoons vinegar

1 teaspoon salt

3 tablespoons lemon juice

1 teaspoon basil

⅛ teaspoon Tabasco sauce, or
to taste

Dissolve the gelatin in the boiling water in a bowl. Add the tomato sauce, vinegar, salt, lemon juice, basil and Tabasco sauce and mix well. Spoon into a mold or shallow dish. Chill, covered, until set. Unmold onto a serving plate. Yields 10 servings.

Hearty Summer Vegetable Salad

florets of ½ head cauliflower

½ bunch broccoli, chopped

2 to 3 ribs celery, thinly sliced

½ cup chopped onion

½ (16-ounce) package
frozen peas

1 cup sour cream

½ cup mayonnaise

½ envelope ranch-style salad
dressing mix

Combine the cauliflower and broccoli in a microwave-safe bowl. Microwave for 5 minutes. Add the celery, onion, peas, sour cream, mayonnaise and salad dressing mix and mix well. Chill, covered, until serving time. Yields 4 servings.

CHAPTER TWO

Hingham Highlights

Meat ~ Chicken ~ Seafood

Cushing Homestead

Matthew Cushing brought his family from Old Hingham, England, to New Hingham in 1638. All who bear the Cushing name in America are descended from him. His son Daniel, a very prominent citizen in his time, was Hingham's third Town Clerk. He recorded the number of settlers who first arrived in Hingham. "The whole number who came out of Norfolk [England] (chiefly from Hingham and vicinity) from 1633 to 1639, and settled in this Hingham, was 206."

Twelve generations of the family have owned and lived in this house. Initially the house consisted of two rooms downstairs and two rooms upstairs. About fifty years after it was built, it was enlarged significantly, so that now it exemplifies two architectural styles of the Colonial period. Although the entire front facade is Georgian, the original kitchen inside the southwest corner is seventeenth-century English style. Restored in 1936, it exhibits the typical painted plaster walls and timbered ceiling, the exposed sills, girts and posts, the shadow molded boards, and cavernous fireplace of Elizabethan England. Some Cushing children in Revolutionary War times carved their initials on a staircase wall.

Baked Cod with Oyster Stuffing

Ye Hingham Cook Book - 1901

Clean a codfish weighing four and one-half pounds, season with salt and pepper and brush over with lemon juice; cut gashes two inches apart on each side, lay over strips of salt pork, skewer and put in a dripping pan, brush over melted butter, dredge with flour, bake in a hot oven one hour, baste often with the hot fat which has tried out of the pork.

Oyster Sauce

Parboil two cups of oysters, melt four tablespoons of butter, add four tablespoons of flour, one-half teaspoon salt, one-half salt spoon of pepper. Pour in the oyster liquor with one and one-quarter cups of milk, add the oysters and reheat. This sauce is equally good for baked cod or boiled turkey.

Special Broiled Flounder

Sampler of Recipes - 1971

½ cup mayonnaise	lemon, salt and pepper
3 tablespoons chopped parsley	to taste
3 tablespoons chopped onions	1 egg white
3 tablespoons not too sour pickles, chopped	2 flounder fillets

Broil in foil 2 flounder fillets. Combine all ingredients except egg white. Beat egg white stiff and fold into mayonnaise mixture. Spread over fillets and place under broiler until light brown. Serve at once. Serves 2.

German Roulins

4 slices bacon, chopped	2 pounds beef, thinly sliced
1 large onion, minced	2 or 3 tablespoons
minced dill pickle to taste	(or more) flour
1 teaspoon prepared mustard	2 teaspoons olive oil
marjoram to taste	2 cups beef broth

Sprinkle the bacon, onion, pickle, mustard and marjoram over the beef slices. Roll the beef to enclose the filling and secure with wooden picks. Coat well with flour. Brown the rolls on all sides in the heated olive oil in a skillet. Remove to a casserole, reserving the drippings. Stir the remaining flour into the drippings. Cook for several minutes, stirring constantly. Stir in the beef broth. Simmer until thickened, stirring constantly. Pour over the beef rolls. Bake at 350 to 375 degrees for 1½ hours or until the beef is tender. Yields 4 to 6 servings.

A Fine Way to Wash Blankets

Three tablespoons of powdered borax to one pint of soft soap. Cover with cold water and let stand overnight. Rinse thoroughly in cold water. Hang out dripping wet by the sides; pins near together. This is for one pair. Put a forceful stream of water from the hose on both sides of blanket while hanging on the line.

—From *Ye Hingham Cook Book*, 1901

Black Forest Beef Stew

1½ pounds beef roast or steak, cut into cubes
¼ cup butter
1 clove of garlic, minced
⅛ teaspoon parsley flakes
½ teaspoon thyme
½ bay leaf, crumbled
½ teaspoon sugar
¼ teaspoon pepper
1 tablespoon wine vinegar

1 can (or more) beer
12 fresh or frozen small white onions
6 small unpeeled potatoes, chopped
2 or 3 carrots, sliced ¼ inch thick
½ to 1 (10-ounce) package frozen peas, or 1 to 2 cups fresh

Brown the beef in half the butter in a heavy saucepan with a lid. Add the garlic, parsley flakes, thyme, bay leaf, sugar, pepper, vinegar and enough beer to cover the meat. Bring to a boil gradually. Reduce the heat and cover. Simmer for 2 hours, adding additional beer if needed for the desired consistency. Sauté the onions in the remaining butter in a skillet. Add to the stew with the potatoes and carrots. Simmer for 45 minutes. Add the peas. Simmer for 15 minutes. Serve with a green salad and beer. Yields 8 servings.

Portuguese Sopas

1 (3-pound) pot roast, cubed
1 (8-ounce) can tomato sauce
1 large onion, sliced
1 clove of garlic, chopped
1 cup mint leaves
2 tablespoons ground cinnamon
1 teaspoon ground cloves
2 teaspoons ground cumin

2 teaspoons allspice
3 bay leaves
1 teaspoon salt
1/2 to 1 teaspoon pepper
1 cup red wine
2 medium heads cabbage
1 loaf French bread, sliced

Combine the beef, tomato sauce, onion, garlic, mint leaves, cinnamon, cloves, cumin, allspice, bay leaves, salt, pepper and red wine with enough water to cover in a large saucepan. Cook over medium heat for 4 hours, adding additional water as needed. Cut each cabbage into quarters. Add to the saucepan. Cook for 30 minutes longer or until the cabbage is tender. Discard the bay leaves. Serve over the French bread. Yields 8 servings.

Sour Cream Meat Loaf

2 eggs
1/4 cup milk
8 ounces sour cream
1/2 cup dry bread crumbs
1/4 cup finely chopped onion
2 tablespoons chopped parsley
1 tablespoon Dijon mustard

1 tablespoon Worcestershire
   sauce
1/4 teaspoon salt
1/4 teaspoon pepper
1 1/2 pounds lean ground beef
1 (3/4-ounce) package brown
   gravy mix

Combine the eggs, milk and half the sour cream in a bowl and
mix well. Stir in the bread crumbs, onion, parsley, mustard, Worcestershire
sauce, salt and pepper. Add the ground beef and mix well.
Press into a greased 5x9-inch loaf pan. Bake at 350 degrees for 1 1/4 hours.
Remove to a serving plate. Let stand for 10 minutes. Prepare the
brown gravy mix with the remaining sour cream using the package
directions. Serve with the meat loaf. Yields 6 servings.

Household Hint

*Curtain and portiere poles allow the hangings to slip easily if rubbed
with hard soap. That is much better than greasing. Creaking doors
and drawers should be treated the same way.*

—From *Ye Hingham Cook Book*, 1901

Braised Lamb Shanks

4 lamb shanks	2 bay leaves
flour	1/4 teaspoon oregano
salt and pepper to taste	minced parsley, rosemary and
1/4 cup olive oil	thyme to taste
1/4 cup chopped onion	1 (10-ounce) can beef consommé
1/4 cup chopped celery	2 tablespoons tomato paste
1/4 cup chopped carrot	1/2 cup red wine
2 cloves of garlic, minced	peas and mushrooms (optional)

Cut the flaps off the lamb shanks and discard. Shake the shanks
in a mixture of flour, salt and pepper, coating well. Brown on all sides
in the heated olive oil in a skillet. Remove to a Dutch oven. Add
the onion, celery, carrot, garlic, bay leaves, oregano, parsley, rosemary
and thyme to the drippings in the skillet. Sauté for 5 minutes.
Add to the Dutch oven with the beef consommé, tomato paste and wine.
Bake at 350 degrees for 1½ hours. Remove the lamb shanks and
cut the meat into cubes, discarding the bones. Return the meat to the
Dutch oven. Add peas and mushrooms. Simmer on the stove
top until tender; discard the bay leaves. Thicken with additional flour
if needed for the desired consistency. Yields 4 to 6 servings.

Greek Burgers

1 pound ground lamb
1 tablespoon minced onion
1 clove of garlic, minced
1 tablespoon Dijon mustard
1 tablespoon lemon juice

½ teaspoon dried rosemary, crushed
½ teaspoon salt
¼ teaspoon pepper

Combine the ground lamb, onion, garlic, mustard, lemon juice, rosemary, salt and pepper in a bowl and mix well. Shape into 4 patties. Grill until cooked through. Serve on buns with sliced cucumbers and tomatoes and a dollop of yogurt. You may also panfry or broil these burgers. Yields 4 servings.

Broccoli and Ham Ring

4 ounces cooked ham
4 ounces fresh broccoli
1 small onion
6 ounces Swiss cheese, coarsely shredded

½ cup finely chopped parsley
2 tablespoons Dijon mustard
1 teaspoon lemon juice
2 (8-count) packages crescent roll dough

Chop the ham, broccoli and onion coarsely. Combine with the cheese, parsley, mustard and lemon juice in a bowl and mix well. Separate the roll dough into triangles. Arrange the triangles in a circle on a 13-inch baking sheet with the points toward the outer edge and wide ends overlapping in the center to leave a circle 3 inches in diameter. Spoon the filling over the wide ends of the triangles. Fold the points over the filling and tuck under at the center; the filling will not be completely covered. Bake at 350 degrees for 25 to 30 minutes or until golden brown. Yields 8 servings.

Mustard Pork with Cherry Tomatoes

1½ pounds pork shoulder, trimmed

2 tablespoons vegetable oil

2 teaspoons chopped fresh rosemary

1 ounce (2 tablespoons) butter

1 pound medium onions, cut into quarters

3 cloves of garlic, crushed

¼ cup tomato paste

4 fluid ounces (½ cup) dry sherry

2 teaspoons flour

1½ cups chicken stock

2 teaspoons dark soy sauce

salt and pepper to taste

1 pound small flat black mushrooms

¼ cup vegetable oil

1 tablespoon whole grain mustard

9 ounces cherry tomatoes

Cut the pork into 1-inch cubes. Combine with 2 tablespoons oil and rosemary in a bowl and mix well. Marinate in the refrigerator for 2 hours. Heat the butter in a Dutch oven just until it begins to color. Add the pork in batches and sauté until golden brown, removing to a bowl with a slotted spoon. Reduce the heat and add the onions to the drippings. Cook for 5 to 7 minutes or until tender and golden brown. Add the garlic and tomato paste. Cook for 2 to 3 minutes. Add the sherry and bring to a boil. Simmer until reduced by half. Stir in the flour. Cook for several minutes, stirring constantly. Add the chicken stock. Simmer until slightly thickened, stirring constantly. Return the pork to the Dutch oven and add the soy sauce, salt and pepper. Simmer for 5 minutes. Bake, tightly covered, at 350 degrees (180 degrees C or Gas mark 4) for 1 hour and 20 minutes or until the pork is tender. Sauté the mushrooms in ¼ cup oil in a large skillet for 3 to 4 minutes. Season to taste and add to the Dutch oven. Bake for 10 minutes longer. Stir in the mustard. Bring to a boil on the stove top. Add the tomatoes. Simmer for 1 to 2 minutes. Serve immediately. Garnish with parsley and additional rosemary. Yields 4 servings.

Note: To freeze this dish, cool before adding the mustard and freeze. Thaw and stir in the mustard. Reheat at 350 degrees for 25 to 30 minutes or until heated through and stir in the tomatoes. Let stand for 5 minutes before serving.

Spaghetti with Veal and Peppers

1½ pounds boneless veal, cubed

½ teaspoon oregano

1 teaspoon salt

¼ teaspoon dried red pepper

3 tablespoons butter

2 tablespoons flour

1 cup beef broth

1½ cups thinly sliced onions

1 clove of garlic, minced

3 to 4 green bell peppers, thinly sliced

¼ cup olive oil

1½ pounds tomatoes, chopped

½ cup marsala or sherry

1 (16-ounce) package spaghetti, cooked

Sauté the veal with the oregano, salt and red pepper in the melted butter in a saucepan. Sprinkle with the flour. Cook for several minutes, stirring constantly. Add the beef broth. Bring to a boil, stirring constantly. Sauté the onions, garlic and green peppers in the olive oil in a skillet until tender. Add to the veal with the tomatoes and wine. Simmer for 30 minutes, stirring occasionally. Serve over the spaghetti. Yields 6 servings.

Baking Hint

If you are baking bread, turn the loaves top side down in the hot tins and let them stand a few minutes. This will make the crust very tender and they will cut easily.

—From *Ye Hingham Cook Book*, 1901

⟨E⟩ Chicken with Apricots

8 ounces dried apricots

1 cup medium-dry white wine

2 boneless chicken breasts

1 tablespoon flour

salt and pepper to taste

1 ounce (2 tablespoons) butter

8 ounces small button mushrooms

1 tablespoon red currant jelly

1 (170-gram or 5-ounce) can
evaporated milk

Combine the apricots with the wine in a bowl. Let stand for 8 hours or longer, or let no-need-to-soak apricots stand for 1 hour. Coat the chicken with a mixture of the flour, salt and pepper. Cook in the melted butter in a skillet for 2 to 3 minutes or until brown on both sides. Add the apricots, wine, mushrooms and jelly. Bring to a boil and reduce the heat. Simmer until the chicken is cooked through and the wine is reduced by half. Add the evaporated milk. Simmer until thickened to the desired consistency, stirring constantly. Serve immediately garnished with colorful vegetables of choice. You may substitute light cream or half-and-half for the evaporated milk. Yields 2 servings.

Household Hint

Cedar sawdust or Scotch snuff sprinkled over the floor before laying down the carpet will protect it from moths.

—From *Ye Hingham Cook Book,* 1901

Quickie Chickie

1 (8-ounce) bottle regular or fat-free French salad dressing
1 (16-ounce) can whole cranberry sauce

1 envelope onion soup mix
8 to 10 boneless skinless chicken breast halves

Combine the salad dressing, cranberry sauce and soup mix in a bowl and mix well. Arrange the chicken in a baking dish. Pour the dressing mixture over the top. Marinate in the refrigerator for 24 hours. Bake at 350 degrees for 45 minutes. Serve with noodles, rice or couscous. This is also a great last-minute dinner if you keep the ingredients on hand and omit the marinating step. Yields 8 to 10 servings.

Lemon Chicken

1½ pounds boneless skinless chicken breast halves
flour
olive oil

1 envelope brown gravy mix
juice of ½ lemon
¼ cup white wine

Pound the chicken with a meat mallet until thin. Coat with flour. Cook in olive oil in a skillet until golden brown; drain. Place in a shallow baking dish. Prepare the gravy mix in a saucepan using the package directions. Add the lemon juice and wine. Simmer for several minutes. Pour over the chicken. Bake at 350 degrees for 30 minutes, basting occasionally. Garnish with thinly sliced lemon and parsley. Yields 4 servings.

Pecan Chicken

2 whole boneless skinless
chicken breasts
salt and pepper to taste
6 tablespoons butter or
margarine

2 tablespoons Dijon mustard
5 or 6 ounces pecans,
finely ground
1 cup sour cream
1 tablespoon Dijon mustard

Slice the chicken crosswise into very thin slices. Pound flat between waxed paper with a meat mallet. Season with salt and pepper. Melt the butter in a medium saucepan and remove from the heat. Whisk in 2 tablespoons mustard. Spread the pecans on waxed paper. Dip the chicken into the butter mixture and coat with the pecans. Arrange in a single layer in an oiled shallow baking dish. Bake at 400 degrees for 8 to 10 minutes or until cooked through. Combine the sour cream and 1 tablespoon mustard in a small saucepan. Bring to a boil and remove from the heat. Place on plates spread with some of the sauce if desired and serve with the remaining sauce. Yields 4 servings.

Chicken and Wild Rice Salad

1 cup uncooked white long grain
and wild rice mix
1/4 cup sliced scallions with
green tops
1/4 teaspoon finely minced
lemon zest
1/2 tablespoon lemon juice

2/3 cup plain low-fat yogurt
3 tablespoons olive oil
1/2 teaspoon salt
freshly ground pepper to taste
2 cups chopped cooked chicken
1 cup chopped walnuts or pecans

Cook the rice using the package directions. Cool to room temperature. Combine the scallions, lemon zest, lemon juice, yogurt, olive oil, salt and pepper in a large bowl and mix well. Stir in the rice, chicken and walnuts. Chill until serving time. Yields 6 servings.

Chicken Transformations

1 pound boneless skinless chicken breasts
1 tablespoon butter or margarine
1 tablespoon olive oil
salt and pepper to taste
1/2 cup (or more) orange juice
chopped Italian parsley

Slice the chicken very thin or pound thin between waxed paper. Heat the butter and olive oil in a large nonstick skillet. Sauté the chicken in a single layer, in batches if necessary, in the oil mixture until light brown. Return the chicken to the skillet and season with salt and pepper. Add the orange juice. Cook until the chicken is cooked through. Remove the chicken to a warm serving platter. Add additional orange juice to the skillet if needed and bring to a boil. Cook until reduced by half or until thickened to the desired consistency. Serve over the chicken; garnish with orange sections and sprinkle with the parsley. Yields 4 servings.

Note: Transform this recipe by substituting dry sherry, dry white wine, dry vermouth, tomato juice, stewed tomatoes or any liquid of your choice for the orange juice and varying the garnish to match.

Chicken and Rice

1 chicken, cut up
3 tablespoons olive oil
1 green bell pepper, finely
    chopped
1 onion, finely chopped
2 cloves of garlic, finely chopped
2 sprigs of parsley, finely chopped
8 tomatoes, chopped, or
1 or 2 (16-ounce) cans
    stewed tomatoes

½ teaspoon pepper
3 tablespoons dry wine
2 cups chicken broth
4 sprigs of dried saffron
1 cup uncooked rice
1 (10-ounce) package frozen tiny
    peas, or 1 can tiny peas
1 (2-ounce) jar pimento,
    cut into strips

Cook the chicken in the olive oil in a heavy saucepan or Dutch oven until light brown. Add the green pepper, onion, garlic and parsley. Cook for several minutes. Add the tomatoes, pepper and wine. Simmer for 10 minutes. Heat the chicken broth in a saucepan. Dissolve the saffron in 1 tablespoon of the hot broth in a small bowl. Add to the remaining broth and stir into the chicken mixture. Bring to a boil and stir in the rice. Simmer, covered, for 30 minutes. Add the peas and cook until heated through. Top with the pimento and serve from the saucepan. Yields 6 servings.

—Adapted from a 1950 Cuban recipe

Skinny Oven-Fried Chicken

1 to 1½ cups plain or seasoned
dry bread crumbs
½ teaspoon each paprika, celery
seeds and dried thyme

8 skinless chicken breasts,
thighs or legs
½ cup plain low-fat yogurt

Mix the bread crumbs, paprika, celery seeds and thyme on
waxed paper. Spread the chicken with yogurt and coat with the bread
crumb mixture. Arrange in a single layer with sides not touching
in a shallow baking dish that has been greased or sprayed with nonstick
cooking spray. Bake at 400 degrees for 45 to 50 minutes or
until golden brown and juices run clear when the chicken is pierced
with a fork. Yields 4 servings.

Chicken Vermouth

8 chicken breasts, thighs or legs
1½ teaspoons salt
½ teaspoon pepper
2 ribs celery, thinly sliced
1 medium onion, thinly sliced

8 cloves of garlic
2 tablespoons chopped parsley
½ cup dry vermouth
¾ cup sour cream

Season the chicken with salt and pepper and place in a 2-quart
baking dish. Add the celery, onion, garlic, parsley and wine. Cover with
2 layers of foil and a lid. Bake at 375 degrees for 1½ hours
without removing the lid. Stir in the sour cream. Serve over rice or
noodles. Yields 4 servings.

Brunswick Stew

4 medium-large potatoes, peeled,
chopped
2 cups chopped cooked or
uncooked chicken
2 cups chopped cooked or
uncooked pork
1 large onion, grated
1 (10-ounce) package frozen corn
1 (10-ounce) package frozen
baby lima beans
1 (28-ounce) can whole
tomatoes, crushed

½ (14-ounce) bottle catsup
1 tablespoon lemon juice
¼ (16-ounce) bottle hickory
smoke barbecue sauce, or
½ teaspoon liquid smoke
2 to 3 tablespoons cider vinegar
1 tablespoon Worcestershire
sauce
Tabasco sauce to taste
2 to 4 cups chicken broth or
chicken stock

Parboil the potatoes in water in a large stockpot for 5 to 10
minutes; drain. Add the chicken, pork, onion, corn and lima beans. Stir
in the tomatoes, catsup, lemon juice, barbecue sauce, vinegar, Worcestershire
sauce, Tabasco sauce and chicken broth. Bring to a boil over
low heat, stirring frequently. Simmer for several hours or until
of the desired consistency, adding additional broth if needed. The flavor
of this stew improves on the second day. It can be made using only
pork or chicken if preferred. Yields 8 servings.

Cornish Game Hen with Port Sauce

1 (1½-pound) Cornish game hen
⅛ teaspoon instant chicken
bouillon
¼ cup hot water
1 tablespoon minced gingerroot
1 tablespoon minced shallot
2 tablespoons no-sugar-added
seedless blackberry jam

1 clove of garlic, minced
1 tablespoon sherry wine vinegar
¼ cup orange juice
2 tablespoons port
¼ teaspoon dried thyme
ground red pepper to taste
1 bay leaf

Rinse the game hen and pat dry, discarding the giblets, skin and excess fat. Split into halves lengthwise and place meaty side up in a 7x11-inch baking dish sprayed with nonfat cooking spray or lined with foil. Dissolve the instant bouillon in the hot water in a bowl. Add the gingerroot, shallot, jam, garlic, vinegar, orange juice, wine, thyme, red pepper and bay leaf; mix well. Pour over the game hen.

Bake, covered, at 350 degrees for 45 minutes or until cooked through. Remove the game hen to a serving dish. Pour the cooking liquid into a saucepan. Cook for 15 minutes or until reduced to ½ cup; discard the bay leaf. Serve with the game hen. Yields 2 servings.

Turkey and Three-Cheese Lasagna

30 ounces nonfat ricotta cheese
1 cup grated nonfat Parmesan
    cheese
1 (10-ounce) package frozen
    chopped spinach, thawed
salt and pepper to taste

2 large eggs, or
    ½ cup egg substitute
1 recipe Turkey Sauce
15 (no-boil) lasagna noodles
4¾ cups shredded low-fat
    mozzarella cheese

Mix the ricotta cheese and ¾ cup Parmesan cheese in a medium bowl. Add the drained spinach, salt, pepper and eggs. Spread ½ cup of the Turkey Sauce in a 9x13-inch baking dish. Arrange ⅓ of the noodles in the prepared dish and spread with half the spinach mixture. Sprinkle with 2 cups of the mozzarella cheese. Add 1½ cups of the Turkey Sauce. Repeat the noodle and spinach layers. Add 1½ cups of the Turkey Sauce and 2 cups of the mozzarella cheese. Arrange the remaining noodles over the layers and top with the remaining Turkey Sauce, mozzarella cheese and Parmesan cheese. Bake, covered, with foil, at 350 degrees for 40 minutes. Bake, uncovered, for 40 minutes longer or until bubbly. Let stand for 15 minutes. Yields 8 servings.

—Turkey Sauce—

1 cup chopped onion
¾ cup chopped peeled carrot
2 tablespoons minced garlic
1 tablespoon olive oil
8 ounces ground lean turkey
1 (28-ounce) can crushed
    tomatoes with added purée

¼ cup tomato paste
1 tablespoon light brown sugar
½ cup chopped fresh basil
1 tablespoon dried oregano
1 bay leaf
½ teaspoon crushed dried
    red pepper

Sauté the onion, carrot and garlic in the olive oil in a large heavy skillet for 12 minutes or until tender. Add the turkey. Cook for 5 minutes, stirring until crumbly. Add the remaining ingredients. Simmer, covered, for 15 minutes or until reduced to about 5 cups. Discard the bay leaf. Cool to room temperature. Yields 5 cups.

Fried Catfish with Chive and Ginger Sauce

3 tablespoons rice vinegar
2 tablespoons light soy sauce
1 tablespoon fresh lime juice
1 tablespoon grated lime peel
1 teaspoon finely grated fresh
ginger
1 small clove of garlic, crushed

2 teaspoons light brown sugar
4 tablespoons chopped chives
2 (6- to 7-ounce) catfish fillets,
skinned
salt and pepper to taste
flour
peanut oil

Whisk the vinegar, soy sauce, lime juice, lime peel, ginger, garlic and brown sugar in a small bowl until well mixed. Stir in 3 tablespoons of the chives. Chill, covered, for up to 24 hours. Press the remaining 1 tablespoon chives onto both sides of the fish fillets. Sprinkle with salt and pepper and coat with flour, shaking off the excess. Heat ¼ inch oil in a large heavy shallow skillet over medium heat. Add the fillets and cook for about 3 minutes on each side or until crisp on the outside and just until opaque on the inside. Drain on paper towels. Place on a serving plate and spoon the sauce over the top. Sprinkle with additional chives.
Serve immediately. Yields 2 servings.

Broiled Fish Steaks

1/3 cup soy sauce
1/4 cup fresh lemon juice
1/2 cup olive oil
2 teaspoons Dijon mustard
1 large clove of garlic, crushed

1 teaspoon grated lemon peel
chopped fresh parsley
3 pounds (1-inch) salmon or
swordfish steaks

Combine the soy sauce, lemon juice, olive oil, mustard, garlic, lemon peel and parsley in a shallow dish and mix well. Pierce both sides of the fish several times with a fork. Add to the marinade, coating well. Marinate, covered, in the refrigerator for 12 hours or longer, piercing occasionally. Heat the broiler very hot. Drain the fish, reserving the marinade. Place the fish on a rack in the broiler pan. Broil for 6 to 8 minutes on each side or until cooked through, brushing occasionally with the reserved marinade. Garnish with lemon wedges. You may also use flounder or halibut in this recipe or cook on a grill if preferred. Yields 6 servings.

Kedgeree

8 ounces uncooked long
grain rice
1 pound smoked haddock,
salmon, cod, turbot, halibut or
other fish

3 eggs
2 ounces butter
salt and pepper to taste
½ cup light cream
milk

Cook the rice until tender using the package directions. Drain and rinse the rice and spread on a clean surface to dry; this prevents the kedgeree from becoming stodgy. Cook the fish with just enough water to cover in a saucepan for 10 to 15 minutes or until tender; drain. Skin and flake the fish, discarding any bones. Boil the eggs in water in a saucepan for 8 minutes or until firm. Plunge into cold water and remove the shells. Chop 1 egg and slice the remaining eggs. Melt the butter in a saucepan. Add the fish, rice and chopped egg. Season with salt and pepper. Cook over medium heat until heated through, stirring constantly. Stir in the cream and enough milk to make of the desired consistency. Spoon into a serving bowl and top with the sliced eggs. Serve hot or cold. Yields 4 servings.

Kedgeree

In the days when large houses had servants and breakfast
was set out on the sideboard, kedgeree was always one of the
dishes served, along with kippers and eggs. The original spicy Indian dish
containing onions and lentils was brought to England and Anglicized, leaving out the
stronger flavors and, in the Eastern Counties, adding flaked smoked fish.
It is believed to be a favorite of the royal family.

Baked Fillet of Sole

2 tablespoons butter	⅔ cup light cream
2 teaspoons flour	salt and pepper to taste
2 teaspoons grated onion	12 (6- to 7-inch) sole fillets
⅔ cup white wine	paprika to taste

Melt the butter in a small saucepan. Stir in the flour and onion. Cook until the flour is blended into the butter, stirring constantly. Add the wine. Cook for 10 minutes, stirring constantly. Stir in the cream, salt and pepper and remove from the heat. Roll the fillets and arrange in a buttered shallow baking dish. Pour the sauce over the top and sprinkle with paprika. Bake, uncovered, at 350 degrees for 30 minutes. You may prepare this dish ahead and chill until time to bake. Yields 6 servings.

Herbes de Provence Mix

Combine 1 tablespoon each of dried marjoram, thyme and savory; 1 teaspoon each of dried basil, rosemary and lavender blossoms; ½ teaspoon each of sage and cracked fennel seeds; and 1 to 2 tablespoons dried parsley in an airtight jar and mix well. Use in omelettes, soups, stews, dips, gravies and chicken dishes.

New England Stuffed Sole

1½ cups bread crumbs
½ cup melted butter
1 tablespoon lemon juice
1 teaspoon soy sauce
1 medium onion, grated
parsley to taste

¼ teaspoon sage
salt and pepper to taste
8 large or 12 small sole or
flounder fillets
2 tablespoons melted butter

Combine the bread crumbs, ½ cup butter, lemon juice, soy sauce, onion, parsley, sage, salt and pepper in a bowl and mix well. Spoon the mixture onto the fish fillets. Roll the fish to enclose the filling and secure with wooden picks. Arrange in a baking dish and drizzle with 2 tablespoons butter. Bake at 350 degrees for 30 minutes. Yields 6 to 8 servings.

Mini Clambake

1 (8-ounce) can minced
clams, drained
8 ounces cream cheese, softened
1 tablespoon grated onion

½ cup mayonnaise
¼ teaspoon celery seeds
salt to taste

Combine the clams, cream cheese, onion, mayonnaise, celery seeds and salt in a bowl and mix well. Spoon into a 1-quart baking dish. Bake, uncovered, at 350 degrees for 30 minutes. Serve with crackers. Yields 4 servings.

Stir-Fried Scallops and Snow Peas

½ cup chicken stock
1 tablespoon cornstarch
2 tablespoons dry sherry
2 tablespoons soy sauce
1 teaspoon minced fresh ginger
1 tablespoon vegetable oil
1 tablespoon minced garlic

4 scallions with green stems,
    sliced diagonally into
    1-inch pieces
1½ cups snow peas, trimmed
1 pound bay scallops or sea
    scallops, cut into quarters, dried
¼ cup coarsely chopped walnuts

Whisk the chicken stock into the cornstarch in a small bowl.
Add the sherry, soy sauce and ginger and mix well. Heat half the oil
in a wok or nonstick skillet over high heat until hot. Add the
garlic, scallions and snow peas. Stir-fry for 2 minutes or until the snow
peas are tender-crisp. Remove to a bowl. Add the remaining oil
and scallops to the wok. Stir-fry for 1 minute. Stir in the chicken stock
mixture. Cook for 1 minute or until slightly thickened, stirring
constantly. Add the snow pea mixture and walnuts. Cook just until
heated through. Serve immediately. Yields 4 servings.

John Quincy Adams

*In 1787 John Quincy Adams attended a grand ball in Hingham, given by
Madame Sarah Derby in honor of Henry Ware, the new pastor of the
old Ship Church. Ware had been Adams's roommate at Harvard. In his diary,
Adams noted that dancing went on until between two and three o'clock in
the morning. The next night, after more dancing and card playing,
"a number of the lads . . . went serenading all
over the town till daylight."*

Scallops and Shrimp with Orzo and Spinach

2 (10-ounce) packages
frozen spinach

2 quarts water

8 ounces bay scallops

8 ounces medium shrimp,
peeled, deveined

1½ cups uncooked orzo

1 teaspoon salt (optional)

6 tablespoons pine nuts

3 tablespoons olive oil

6 cloves of garlic,
minced or crushed

5 tablspoons minced
sun-dried tomato

¼ cup dry white wine

¾ cup grated Parmesan cheese

salt and pepper to taste

Drain the spinach in a colander and press with the back of a spoon to remove excess liquid. Bring 2 quarts water to a boil in a medium saucepan. Add the scallops and shrimp. Cover and remove from the heat. Let stand for 8 minutes or until opaque. Remove to a warm bowl with a slotted spoon. Bring the water to a boil again and add the orzo and 1 teaspoon salt. Cook for 8 to 10 minutes or until tender; drain and keep warm. Toast the pine nuts in a large heated saucepan over medium heat for 6 minutes or until golden brown, stirring frequently. Remove to a bowl. Heat the oil in the same saucepan and add the garlic and sun-dried tomato. Cook for 1 minute or until tender. Add the spinach and pasta. Cook until heated through, stirring constantly. Stir in the wine. Add the seafood, pine nuts and cheese. Season to taste with salt and pepper. This is even better reheated, or can be served cold. Yields 6 servings.

Baked Scallops

2 pounds scallops
1 roll (about) butter
    crackers, crushed
½ cup melted butter
¼ cup sherry
1 teaspoon chopped parsley

Clean the scallops and place in a baking dish. Mix the cracker crumbs with the melted butter, sherry and parsley in a bowl. Sprinkle over the scallops. Bake, covered with foil, at 350 degrees for 40 minutes. Yields 6 to 8 servings.

Shrimp Fettuccini

1 (16-ounce) package fettuccini
1 medium onion, chopped
1 tablespoon chopped parsley
¼ cup butter
4 ounces tomato sauce
2 cups whipping cream
8 ounces portobello
    mushrooms, sliced
1 pound shrimp, peeled, deveined
1 cup grated Parmesan cheese

Cook the fettuccini using the package directions; rinse, drain and keep warm. Sauté the onion and parsley in the butter in a large saucepan over low heat until the onion is tender. Add the tomato sauce and cream. Bring to a boil. Stir in the mushrooms and shrimp. Cook until the shrimp are pink. Add the pasta and cheese and toss lightly to mix well. Serve immediately. Yields 4 servings.

Baked Shrimp and Feta Cheese with Fresh Basil and Tomatoes

6 ounces feta cheese

1½ teaspoons vegetable oil

⅓ cup chopped onion

1 tablespoon minced garlic

2 cups chopped seeded
plum tomatoes

¼ cup chopped fresh parsley

2 tablespoons chopped fresh
basil, or ¼ teaspoon dried

1 tablespoon chopped fresh
marjoram, or ¼ tablespoon
dried

1 teaspoon julienned fresh lemon
zest or peel

freshly ground allspice and
pepper to taste

1 pound large shrimp,
peeled, deveined

Crumble the cheese into 1-inch pieces and drain. Heat a small flameproof baking dish over medium heat and add the oil. Sauté the onion in the heated oil for 3 minutes or until tender but not brown. Add the garlic and sauté for 30 seconds or until pungent but not brown. Add the tomatoes, parsley, basil, marjoram and lemon zest. Simmer over low heat for 10 minutes, stirring occasionally. Season to taste with allspice and pepper. Remove from the heat; the mixture will appear dry. Arrange the shrimp in the baking dish and sprinkle with the cheese. Bake at 400 degrees for 12 to 15 minutes or until the shrimp are cooked through; the moisture in the shrimp and cheese will make a light sauce. Yields 4 servings.

Marinated Shrimp Kabobs

3½ tablespoons unsalted butter

3 tablespoons olive oil

3 tablespoons chili sauce

1 tablespoon
Worcestershire sauce

¼ tablespoon Tabasco sauce

1 tablespoon lemon juice

2 cloves of garlic, crushed

1 tablespoon chopped
fresh parsley

½ tablespoon oregano

¾ tablespoon cayenne

salt and black pepper to taste

1 pound uncooked shrimp,
peeled, with tails intact

Combine the butter, olive oil, chili sauce, Worcestershire sauce, Tabasco sauce, lemon juice, garlic, parsley, oregano, cayenne, salt and pepper in a saucepan. Cook over medium heat until the flavors blend, stirring constantly. Cool to room temperature. Combine with the shrimp in a covered container. Marinate in the refrigerator for 2 to 3 hours. Drain, reserving the marinade. Thread the shrimp onto skewers. Grill until cooked through, basting with the reserved marinade. Yields 2 servings.

Savory Sidelines

Meatless Main Dishes — Vegetables — Side Dishes

Old Ship Meetinghouse

    Most seventeenth-century New England towns were ecclesiastical parishes, with the meetinghouse the dominant structure and the minister the acknowledged leader. After the death of Peter Hobart, Hingham's first minister, the parishioners decided that the First Parish Church, built in 1635, could no longer serve the needs of the community.

    Old Ship Meetinghouse was erected in 1681, and is the oldest meetinghouse in the country, with services held regularly since its dedication on January 8, 1682. A national Historic Landmark, it is also the only surviving example of the English Gothic style of the seventeenth century in this country.

    The lofty curved oak timbers supporting the ceiling soar above the pews and high pulpit and resemble an upside-down ship's keel, hence the name "Old Ship." A copy of the ceiling is on display in the American Wing of the Metropolitan Museum of Art in New York. The original interior was restored in 1930 by Eben Howard Gay, a descendent of the Reverend Ebenezer Gay, the third minister of the parish, who served for seventy years.

Bean Porridge
Ye Hingham Cook Book - 1901

Soak over night one pint of small white beans. In the morning pour off
the water and put the beans on a slow fire in two quarts of fresh water.
Add two and a half pounds of fat corned beef and a small piece of salt pork.
Let it simmer gently for a day and a half, taking out the beef when it
becomes tender. Strain, and serve with toast.

Prune-Noodles With Almonds
Sampler of Recipes - 1971

6 cooked prunes (or more)   ½ cup toasted,
        1 cup flat noodles   blanched almonds
        3 tablespoons butter

Cook noodles (use wide flat ones) until tender in salted water.
Drain thoroughly. Saute noodles in butter in fry pan until brown—turn once.
Add prunes (no juice) and heat. Sprinkle with almonds when served. Serves 2.

End-of-the-Garden Pasta

4 cups chopped fresh vegetables

4 cups boiling water

3 to 4 tablespoons butter or margarine

1 small tomato, crushed, or

2 tablespoons tomato paste

1½ cups chicken stock

1 pound spaghetti or small shell or spiral pasta

1 tablespoon chopped Italian parsley

½ cup grated Parmesan cheese

salt and pepper to taste

Blanch the chopped vegetables in the boiling water in a large saucepan for 2 minutes. Drain and rinse with cold water. Melt the butter in a large skillet. Add the blanched vegetables and sauté for 3 to 4 minutes or until tender-crisp. Add the tomato and chicken stock. Bring to a boil and cook until reduced by half. Cook the pasta using the package directions; drain. Add to the vegetables. Cook for 1 minute. Add the parsley, cheese, salt and pepper; toss lightly to mix well. Serve immediately. Yields 4 main course servings or 6 side dish servings.

Note: You may use whatever vegetables are left in the garden or are in season for this dish, such as zucchini, summer squash, carrots, scallions, bell peppers, spinach or chard.

Garden Hint

If you cultivate raspberries and blackberries, have sawdust from the woodhouse put around them once a year. Where these berries grow wild, the largest ones are found near decayed stumps and logs.

—From *Ye Hingham Cook Book,* 1901

Pasta with Three Cheeses

6 cups chopped ripe summer
tomatoes
1 clove of garlic, minced
½ to 1 (4-ounce) can chopped
mild green chiles
½ cup olive oil
½ cup coarsely chopped
fresh basil

salt and pepper to taste
1 pound rigatoni, ribbed
ziti or farfalle
½ cup grated Parmesan cheese
½ cup Gorgonzola or bleu
cheese, crumbled
½ cup grated Danish
fontina cheese

Combine the tomatoes with the garlic, green chiles, olive oil, basil, salt and pepper in a large bowl. Let stand at room temperature for 1 hour or longer. Cook the pasta al dente using the package directions; drain. Combine with half the olive oil drained from the tomato mixture in a large pasta bowl; toss to coat well. Add the Parmesan and Gorgonzola cheeses and toss. Stir the fontina cheese into the tomato mixture. Spoon over the pasta and toss at the table. Serve warm or at room temperature rather than hot. Yields 3 to 4 main course servings or 6 side dish servings.

Note: This dish is only good with fresh summer tomatoes. Canned or winter tomatoes don't work as well, so enjoy it in late summer and hope for a short winter.

Stuffed Peppers

4 large green bell peppers
1 large eggplant, peeled, chopped
2 tablespoons olive oil
2 cups chopped canned tomatoes
12 anchovies, finely chopped
2 cloves of garlic, finely chopped

1½ ounces capers, chopped
2 tablespoons chopped parsley
2½ cups fresh bread crumbs
3 ounces Parmesan cheese, grated
nutmeg, salt and pepper to taste
5 tablespoons olive oil

Cut the peppers into halves, discarding the seeds and membranes. Sauté the eggplant in 2 tablespoons olive oil in a skillet until tender; remove from the heat and cool. Combine the tomatoes, anchovies, garlic, capers and parsley in a bowl. Add the bread crumbs, eggplant, cheese, nutmeg, salt and pepper and mix well. Spoon into the pepper halves and place in an oiled baking pan. Drizzle with 5 tablespoons olive oil. Bake at 400 degrees for 30 minutes. Yields 4 servings.

Wars

Many men from Hingham fought in the Revolution, foremost among them General Benjamin Lincoln, whose house still stands on North Street. Lincoln served as a colonel in the 2nd Militia Regiment, which went to Lexington and Concord. In February of 1776, he planned and commanded the successful movement that finally drove the enemy from Boston Harbor. Not all Hingham citizens supported the revolutionaries, however. Shipowner Martin Gay joined the evacuation of General Howe and his British soldiers from Boston to Halifax, taking with him his daughter and son, "his man London," and his favorite secretary bookcase, which was later named the "Tory Desk." During the Civil War, Solomon Lincoln observed that Hingham citizens reacted with "the same courage which supported our fathers through the weary years of the Revolution." Hundreds of Hingham men enlisted; over eighty died.

Quiche

1 cup steamed spinach,
well drained
½ cup sliced cherry tomatoes
4 slices crisp-fried bacon,
crumbled (optional)
3 large mushrooms, sliced
1 unbaked (9-inch) pie shell

½ cup shredded Monterey
Jack cheese
½ cup shredded mild Cheddar
cheese
6 eggs
½ cup milk or cream

Combine the spinach, tomatoes, bacon and mushrooms in a bowl
and mix well. Spoon into the pie shell and sprinkle with the cheeses. Beat
the eggs lightly with the milk in a bowl. Pour over the spinach mixture. Bake
at 350 degrees for 1 hour or until set. Yields 6 servings.

The Cheese State

In the early nineteenth century in Hingham, Wisconsin, farm work was done
by oxen, as there were no horses or buggies. Mail was carried on foot between Milwaukee
and Green Bay, and the carrier made the trip once a month. There were no highways
at that time, only cow paths marked by blazed trees through the woods. About thirty
families joined together to go by turns for the mail. Sheep raising was one
of the principal occupations in the early days. Sheepshearing festivals were held in
the village, with a prize for the one who could shear a sheep the best and
quickest. Later, dairying became the chief industry, and the first cheese factories
began production in what would become known as "the cheese state."

Vegetarian Curry

3 cloves of garlic, minced
2 tablespoons olive oil
1 large onion, chopped
1 teaspoon ground coriander
1 teaspoon ground cumin
1 teaspoon ground turmeric
½ teaspoon (scant) ground cloves
½ teaspoon ground cinnamon
⅓ teaspoon ground ginger
¼ teaspoon cayenne, or to taste

1½ cups dried red or off-white lentils
3 to 4 cups vegetable stock made from bouillon cubes
2 unpeeled apples, chopped
3 medium carrots, cubed
3 tablespoons dark raisins or golden raisins
1 (16-ounce) can pineapple cubes
red and/or green bell peppers, chopped (optional)

Sauté the garlic in the heated olive oil in a large skillet for 1½ minutes or until tender. Add the onion. Cook for 2 to 3 minutes or until tender but not brown. Stir in the coriander, cumin, turmeric, cloves, cinnamon, ginger and cayenne. Cook for 3 to 4 minutes. Rinse and sort the lentils. Add the lentils to the skillet. Cook for 2 to 3 minutes, stirring frequently. Add the vegetable stock, apples, carrots, raisins, undrained pineapple and bell peppers. Cook, covered, for 25 minutes or until the lentils are tender, stirring occasionally. Serve with rice and mango chutney. Yields 4 servings.

Pennsylvania German-Style Broccoli

4 slices bacon

1 pound broccoli, chopped

4 scallions

1 medium red bell pepper, chopped

1/3 cup cider vinegar

4 teaspoons spicy brown mustard

3/4 teaspoon sugar

3/4 teaspoon salt

1/2 teaspoon pepper

2 tablespoons vegetable oil

Cook the bacon in a medium skillet over medium heat for 10 minutes or until crisp. Drain and crumble the bacon; drain the skillet, reserving 3 tablespoons of the drippings. Return the reserved drippings to the skillet and set the skillet aside. Steam the broccoli in a steamer for 8 minutes or until tender-crisp. Combine with the scallions and bell pepper in a serving bowl. Reheat the bacon drippings in the skillet over medium heat. Add the vinegar, mustard, sugar, salt and pepper. Cook until heated through, stirring to deglaze the skillet. Remove from the heat and stir in the oil. Pour over the vegetables and toss to mix well. Sprinkle with the crumbled bacon and serve immediately. Yields 6 servings.

Note: You may microwave the broccoli with 1 tablespoon water on High for 5 minutes or until tender-crisp. The bacon and dressing can be prepared in advance, reheating the dressing at serving time.

Carrots and Cranberries

4 cups grated carrots
1 Granny Smith or other tart
apple, grated
1 cup fresh cranberries

½ cup apple juice or cider
3 tablespoons brown sugar
½ teaspoon salt
2 tablespoons butter

Combine the carrots and apple with the cranberries, apple juice, brown sugar and salt in a bowl and mix well. Spoon into a 2-quart baking dish and dot with the butter. Bake, covered, at 350 degrees for 40 minutes. Serve with turkey or roast pork for the holidays. Yields 4 to 6 servings.

Baked Mushroom-Stuffed Onions

12 medium onions
8 ounces fresh mushrooms,
chopped
1 teaspoon finely chopped pecans

3 tablespoons butter
salt and pepper to taste
1 cup chicken consommé
paprika to taste

Pour boiling water over the onions and slip off the skins. Remove and chop the cores, leaving ½-inch shells. Cook the shells in water to cover in a saucepan until nearly tender; invert to drain. Sauté the chopped onion cores, mushrooms and pecans in the butter in a skillet for 10 minutes. Season with salt and pepper. Spoon into the onion shells and arrange in a shallow baking pan. Pour the consommé around the onions and sprinkle lightly with paprika. Bake at 350 degrees for 10 minutes or until light brown and tender. Yields 6 servings.

—From *Sampler of Recipes,* 1971

Swedish-Style Baked Potatoes

8 medium potatoes
¼ cup butter
salt to taste
¼ cup fine bread crumbs

½ cup grated nonfat Parmesan cheese or shredded Swiss cheese

Peel the potatoes, wash and dry well. Cut crosswise into thin slices, cutting to but not through the bottoms. Melt half the butter in an earthenware or baking dish large enough to hold the potatoes. Add the potatoes, turning to coat well with the butter. Dot with the remaining butter and sprinkle with salt. Bake at 500 degrees for 10 minutes, basting with the butter 2 or 3 times. Sprinkle with the cheese and bread crumbs. Bake for 25 minutes longer or until tender; do not baste. Serve immediately. Yields 8 servings.

To Clean Gilded Frames

Gilded frames can be cleaned by gently wiping them with a fine cotton cloth dipped in sweet oil. In the summer when flies are troublesome wash the frames in water in which two or three onions have been boiled. This will not deaden the gilding, but insures for them a good luster.

—From *Ye Hingham Cook Book*, 1901

No-Shell Peas

1 pound unshelled tender   3 quarts boiling water
green peas

Wash the peas, leaving in the shells. Cook in water in a saucepan
for 10 minutes or until the peas are tender; test by removing
1 pea shell and gently pressing the peas to see if they are cooked
through. Drain and serve. To eat, place the pea shell in the mouth and
gently slide through the teeth to press out the peas, discarding
the pods. Yields 4 servings.

Note: This easy recipe avoids shelling the peas. It is best in the
spring when fresh peas are at their peak. Do not use pea pods or
sugar snap peas as a substitute.

Squash and Apple Casserole

1¼ pounds butternut squash   ¼ teaspoon cinnamon
4 to 5 apples, peeled, sliced   ¼ teaspoon nutmeg
½ cup packed brown sugar   1 teaspoon salt
1 tablespoon flour   ¼ cup chilled margarine

Cut the squash into 1-inch pieces. Combine with the apples
in a 9x13-inch baking dish. Mix the brown sugar, flour, cinnamon, nutmeg
and salt in a bowl. Cut in the margarine until crumbly. Sprinkle
over the squash mixture. Bake, covered with foil, at 350 degrees for
50 to 60 minutes or until tender. Yields 8 servings.

Summer Squash Casserole

1 onion, chopped
1 clove of garlic, finely minced
1 tablespoon olive oil
1 teaspoon dried oregano, or
2 teaspoons chopped fresh
salt and pepper to taste
2 medium zucchini, sliced

2 medium yellow summer squash
1 cup chopped peeled fresh
tomatoes or drained canned
Italian plum tomatoes
½ cup grated Parmesan cheese
½ cup fine fresh bread crumbs
2 tablespoons butter

Sauté the onion and garlic in the heated olive oil in an ovenproof skillet until tender but not brown. Add the oregano. Cook for 2 minutes; sprinkle with salt and pepper. Add the squash. Sauté for several minutes. Stir in the tomatoes. Bake at 400 degrees for 20 minutes. Mix the cheese and bread crumbs in a bowl. Stir half the cheese mixture gently into the squash; sprinkle the remaining cheese mixture over the top. Dot with the butter. Reduce the oven temperature to 350 degrees. Bake for 45 minutes longer. Yields 4 to 6 servings.

Island Squash Casserole

2 each medium zucchini and
yellow squash, peeled, sliced
½ cup margarine, softened
2 eggs, beaten
¼ cup chopped onion
¼ cup chopped green
bell pepper

½ cup mayonnaise
1 tablespoon sugar or equivalent
amount of sugar substitute
½ cup shredded Cheddar cheese
20 saltines, crushed
seasoned stuffing mix
paprika to taste

Cook the squash in water in a saucepan until tender; drain. Mix with the next 8 ingredients in a bowl. Spoon into an ungreased baking dish or loaf pan. Top with a mixture of the stuffing mix and paprika. Bake at 350 degrees for 30 to 45 minutes or until bubbly. Yields 8 servings.

Sweet Potatoes in Sherry Sauce

1 (16-ounce) can sweet
potatoes, drained
salt to taste
½ cup packed brown sugar
1 tablespoon cornstarch
½ teaspoon salt

1 cup orange juice
½ cup golden raisins
2 tablespoons sherry
2 tablespoons chopped walnuts
½ teaspoon grated orange peel

Arrange the sweet potatoes in a 1½-quart baking dish and sprinkle with salt to taste. Combine the brown sugar, cornstarch and ½ teaspoon salt in a saucepan. Stir in the orange juice; add the raisins. Bring to a boil over high heat, stirring constantly. Stir in the wine, walnuts and orange peel. Pour over the sweet potatoes. Bake at 350 degrees for 25 to 30 minutes or until the sweet potatoes are glazed. Yields 4 servings.

Peter Hobart

In the early 1630s, Reverend Peter Hobart led a company of settlers, seeking the freedom to worship and govern themselves, from Norfolk, England, to America. After stopping briefly in Charlestown, they came to what was then called Bare Cove, now Hingham. Other settlers had preceded them, but it was Hobart's company who formed the core of the new plantation. The economy of the new town was supported by farmers raising corn and salt meadow and fresh meadow hay, as well as by blacksmiths, wheelwrights, and coopers. During the eighteenth century, the town continued to prosper with the establishment of gristmills, sawmills, an ironworks, a shipbuilding yard, and several large fishing fleets.

Autumn Green Tomato Casserole

3 cups sliced green tomatoes
salt and pepper to taste
3 eggs or equivalent
amount of egg substitute
1/2 cup milk

1/4 cup chopped pimento
1/2 cup nonfat cottage cheese
1 teaspoon each chopped fresh
oregano and basil, or
1/2 teaspoon dried

Arrange the tomato slices in a 9-inch pie plate brushed with oil or sprayed with nonstick cooking spray. Season to taste with salt and pepper. Beat the eggs with the milk, pimento, cottage cheese, oregano and basil in a bowl. Pour over the tomatoes. Bake at 375 degrees for 40 minutes. Yields 4 servings.

Roasted Vegetables with Onion and Garlic

4 to 6 tablespoons
olive oil
1 pound fresh green
beans, trimmed
1 red bell pepper, thinly sliced
1 medium yellow or red onion,
thinly sliced

cloves of 1 head of garlic,
peeled, sliced into halves
lengthwise
1/2 teaspoon (scant) salt
2 to 3 tablespoons balsamic
vinegar
freshly ground pepper to taste

Brush a large baking sheet with 2 tablespoons of the olive oil. Pat the green beans dry. Spread the green beans, bell pepper, onion and garlic on the prepared baking sheet. Sprinkle with salt and drizzle with the remaining olive oil. Roast at 400 degrees for 20 to 25 minutes or until the vegetables test tender, shaking the baking sheet several times. Spoon into a serving bowl. Drizzle with the vinegar and sprinkle with pepper. Serve hot, cold or at room temperature. Yields 4 servings.

Rice Pilaf

1 cup uncooked white rice
1 tablespoon olive oil
2½ cups chicken stock

½ cup coarsely chopped walnuts
or pecans

Sauté the rice in the heated olive oil in a large skillet until light brown and slightly puffed; do not overbrown. Bring the chicken stock to a boil in a large saucepan. Add the rice gradually. Cook, covered, over low heat for 30 minutes. Let stand, covered, if necessary until all the liquid is absorbed. Stir in the walnuts. Serve with chicken or pork. You may freeze this dish and reheat in the microwave. Yields 4 servings.

Scented Geranium Rice

2 cups uncooked basmati rice
2 tablespoons unsalted butter
2 teaspoons salt
4 cups water

2 to 4 tablespoons finely
chopped lemon geranium leaves
1 tablespoon coarsely chopped
hollyhock petals (optional)

Bring the rice, butter and salt to a boil with the water in a saucepan and stir once. Reduce the heat to very low. Simmer, covered, for 15 minutes. Place the geranium leaves in a serving bowl. Add the rice and mix well. Let stand for 10 minutes and fluff with a fork. Add the hollyhock petals and toss to mix. Yields 8 to 10 servings.

Risotto with Herbs

5 shallots, chopped
1 clove of garlic, chopped
¼ cup olive oil
2 cups uncooked arborio rice
¼ teaspoon each dried thyme,
rosemary and sage, or
½ teaspoon chopped fresh

salt to taste
6 cups chicken, beef or
vegetable stock
⅔ cup grated Parmesan cheese

Sauté the shallots and garlic in the heated olive oil in a large saucepan until golden brown. Add the rice, thyme, rosemary, sage and salt, stirirng constantly just until the rice begins to brown; do not let burn. Add 1 cup of the stock. Cook until the liquid is absorbed, stirring constantly. Add the remaining stock 1 cup at a time, cooking until the liquid is absorbed after each addition. Cook for a total of 30 to 45 minutes or until the rice is tender. Toss lightly with the cheese in a serving dish. Yields 4 main dish servings or 8 side dish servings.

Household Hints

To keep jellies from moulding, cover with pulverized sugar to the depth of one-quarter of an inch. They will keep for years.

A cloth wet in vinegar and wrapped around cheese will prevent it from moulding. Wrap dry cloth outside of this to keep moisture in.

—From *Ye Hingham Cook Book*, 1901

Cheesy Wild Rice Casserole

1 (6-ounce) package long grain
and wild rice mix
1 (4-ounce) can
mushrooms, drained
2 teaspoons prepared mustard
1/2 teaspoon salt
3/4 cup chopped onion

1 (10-ounce) package frozen
chopped spinach
1 tablespoon butter or margarine
2 1/4 cups water
1/8 teaspoon nutmeg
8 ounces cream cheese, chopped

Combine the rice, seasoning packet, mushrooms, mustard and salt in a
2-quart baking dish. Combine the onion, spinach, butter and water in a medium
saucepan. Bring to a boil, stirring to separate the spinach. Pour over the
rice mixture and add the nutmeg; mix gently. Bake, tightly covered, at 375 degrees
for 30 minutes. Add the cream cheese and mix well. Bake, uncovered, for
10 to 15 minutes longer or until bubbly. Yields 4 main course
servings or 6 to 8 side dish servings.

Household Hint

*Water bottles and vases that become discolored and dirty should have
a new potato cut in bits and put inside with a teaspoon each of salt and washing
soda and two of water. Shake well and rinse in clear water.*

—From *Ye Hingham Cook Book*, 1901

CHAPTER FOUR

Complements with Character

Breads ~ Accompaniments

Second Parish Church

The church building of the Second Parish was raised in 1742 by a group of South Hingham residents. The meetinghouse was, at first, a simple towerless structure with an entrance on the broad south side. In 1792, a square bell tower was added, and in 1829, the galleries were reoriented, a new front bay and belfry added, and the pews decorated by "graining." It stands in a beautiful stretch of broad, tree-lined street, bounded on each side by gracious old homes, in an area known as Glad Tidings Plain, probably "because, thanks to the Indians, it was in the earliest days an open, fertile area where the settlers could grow their crops without first having to cut down the primeval forest."

The first church covenant had no creed beyond "our serious belief of the Christian religion as it is taught in the Bible." In 1836, when denominationalism was beginning to be a factor in town life, it was voted that the minister should be free to "exchange with ministers of all denominations, particularly with those of this town." The following year it was resolved that "Christians of all denominations ought to fellowship together," and in 1846, members declared that it had "never seen fit to deviate at any subsequent time" from that opinion.

Pumpkin Chips

Ye Hingham Cook Book - 1901

Slice the pumpkin all alike about two inches long and one wide, thickness about one-eighth of an inch. Add one pound of sugar to each of pumpkin, the juice of one lemon to each pound of ingredients; a few slices of lemon. Boil until the pumpkin is clear and transparent, then take out the pumpkin and let syrup boil until clear and thick. Put together in jars.

Allen Bluebarry Cake

Sampler of Recipes - 1971

1/3 cup butter	2 cups flour
1/2 cup sugar	2 teaspoons rounded,
pinch of salt	baking powder
dash of nutmeg	1/2 cup blueberries
1 cup milk	

Cream butter and sugar. Add salt and nutmeg. Add milk. Mix. Add flour and baking powder. Mix. Add blueberries. Stir as little as possible to avoid crushing berries. Batter will be quite stiff. Smooth into a greased 9x9x2" pan. Use as a bread.

Grammer's Corn Bread

2 cups stone-ground white
cornmeal, sifted
½ cup flour
2½ teaspoons baking powder
1 teaspoon (or less) salt
1 egg
¼ cup water

¼ cup hot bacon drippings or
vegetable oil
¼ teaspoon baking soda
¼ cup warm water
⅔ cup buttermilk
¼ cup vegetable oil

Sift the cornmeal, flour, baking powder and salt into a bowl. Beat the egg
with ¼ cup water. Add the bacon drippings and mix well. Dissolve
the baking soda in ¼ cup warm water. Add the egg mixture, baking soda
mixture and buttermilk to the cornmeal mixture and mix well. Heat
the oil in a 9- or 10-inch cast-iron skillet in a 450-degree oven. Pour the
batter into the skillet. Bake at 450 degrees for 20 to 25 minutes
or until golden brown. Yields 8 servings.

Corn Oysters

*Six ears of grated corn, one-half cup milk, one-half cup flour, one egg, one
teaspoon of pepper, one teaspoon of salt. Fry on a griddle in small cakes.*

—From *Ye Hingham Cook Book,* 1901

Apricot Nut Bread

1½ cups chopped dried apricots
½ cup butter, softened
1 cup sugar
2 eggs, beaten
¾ cup orange juice
2 cups sifted flour

1 tablespoon baking powder
¼ teaspoon baking soda
¾ teaspoon salt
1 teaspoon grated orange peel
1 cup chopped walnuts

Soak the apricots in water to cover in a bowl for 30 minutes; drain and chop. Cream the butter and sugar in a mixer bowl until light and fluffy. Add the eggs alternately with the orange juice, beating well after each addition. Add the flour, baking powder, baking soda and salt and mix well. Stir in the apricots, orange peel and walnuts. Spoon into two 5x9-inch loaf pans lined with baking parchment. Bake at 350 degrees for 45 minutes. Cool in the pans for several minutes. Remove to a wire rack to cool completely. Yields 2 loaves.

Quick and Easy Tea Bread

2 eggs	1½ cups flour
1 cup sugar	½ cup (or more) fresh
½ cup canola oil	strawberries, raspberries or
¼ cup milk	blueberries
1 teaspoon baking powder	½ cup chopped walnuts
¼ teaspoon baking soda	¼ cup confectioners' sugar
½ teaspoon salt	1 tablespoon boiling water

Beat the eggs with the sugar in a mixer bowl for 1 minute. Add the oil and beat for 1 minute longer. Combine the milk, baking powder, baking soda and salt in a small bowl and beat until smooth. Add to the egg mixture and beat at low speed for 30 seconds. Add the flour and beat for 30 seconds. Fold in the strawberries and walnuts. Spoon into a loaf pan that has been greased and dusted with confectioners' sugar. Bake at 325 degrees for 45 to 55 minutes or until the bread tests done. Cool in the pan for several minutes. Remove to a wire rack to cool. Glaze with a mixture of the confectioners' sugar and boiling water. The flavor improves if the bread is refrigerated overnight. Yields 1 loaf.

Variation: Substitute ⅓ cup lemon juice and ⅓ cup poppy seeds for the berries and walnuts.

Broad Cove Banana Bread

½ cup margarine, softened

1 cup sugar

2 eggs

1½ cups flour

1 teaspoon baking soda

½ teaspoon salt, or to taste

1 cup mashed ripe bananas

½ cup low-fat vanilla yogurt

½ teaspoon vanilla extract

¾ cup chopped walnuts, pecans
    or hazelnuts

Cream the margarine and sugar in a mixer bowl until light and fluffy. Beat in the eggs. Mix the flour, baking soda and salt together. Add to the creamed mixture and mix well. Stir in the bananas, yogurt, vanilla and walnuts. Spoon into a greased 5x9-inch loaf pan. Bake at 350 degrees for 1 hour or until a wooden tester inserted in the center of the bread comes out clean. Cool in the pan for 20 minutes. Remove to a wire rack to cool completely. Yields 1 loaf.

Military Precautions

Early settlements were by necessity little more than military provinces whose armed forces were their own citizens. The picture of the Pilgrim fathers on their way to church with their muskets is a familiar one, but it is not generally known that the law decreed that a man must come armed with musket, powder, and ball to all public assemblies and forbade anyone going unarmed to any place beyond a mile from his dwelling place.

Carrot Bread

¾ cup vegetable oil
1 cup sugar
2 eggs
1½ cups flour
1 teaspoon baking soda

1 teaspoon cinnamon
1 teaspoon salt
1 cup grated carrot
½ cup chopped nuts

Combine the oil, sugar and eggs in a mixer bowl and beat until thick and pale yellow. Add the flour, baking soda, cinnamon and salt and beat until smooth. Stir in the carrot and nuts. Spoon into a greased and floured 5x9-inch loaf pan. Bake at 350 degrees for 55 minutes. Cool in the pan for several minutes. Remove to a wire rack to cool completely. Yields 1 loaf.

Reminiscences

In 1935 Miss May E. Gardner and Mrs. Jennie Cahh Buscher reminisced about their young days in Hingham, Wisconsin. There was a dance hall that attracted folks from miles around. It had a band from Sheboygan and a room with tables piled high with roast turkey, pyramid cakes, and other delicacies. Singing school and spelling schools were the other chief amusements during the long winter evenings. On one corner stood "a very fine drug store" owned by Lyman T. Coller, who was also the country doctor. He administered to the sick for miles around, "often hiring out a team and going on foot to see his patients during the winter season and over bad roads."

Carrot Bran Muffins

3 cups flour
1½ tablespoons baking powder
1 teaspoon baking soda
1 tablespoon cinnamon
½ teaspoon salt (optional)
2 cups bran
4 eggs

1½ cups vegetable oil
1¼ cups packed dark brown
  sugar
¼ cup molasses
3 cups finely grated carrots
1 cup raisins, dates or currants

Sift the flour, baking powder, baking soda, cinnamon and salt together. Stir in the bran. Beat the eggs in a mixer bowl. Add the oil, brown sugar and molasses and beat until smooth. Add the flour mixture and mix well. Stir in the carrots and raisins. Fill greased large muffin cups ¾ full. Bake at 350 degrees for 20 to 25 minutes or until the muffins test done. Yields 2 dozen.

Bucket Town

Hingham buckets were widely known in New England in the nineteenth century. Crocker and Alden Wilder formed the C. & A. Wilder Company, the first to make buckets with brass hoops. At this time, there were so many pail and bucket manufacturers that Hingham became known as "Bucket Town." Hingham buckets can still be seen in antique stores in the area.

Craisin Oatmeal Muffins

1 egg	1 teaspoon baking powder
1 cup buttermilk	½ teaspoon baking soda
½ cup packed brown sugar	½ teaspoon salt (optional)
¼ cup margarine, softened	½ cup craisins (dried cranberries),
1 cup soy or all-purpose flour	raisins or chopped nuts
1 cup quick-cooking oats	

Beat the egg in a mixer bowl. Add the buttermilk, brown sugar and margarine and mix well. Add the flour, oats, baking powder, baking soda and salt; mix just until moistened. Stir in the craisins. Fill paper-lined muffin cups ⅔ full. Bake at 400 degrees for 20 to 25 minutes or until light brown. Remove from the muffin cups immediately.
These muffins freeze well. Yields 1 dozen.

Good Hard Soap

One can Babbitt's lye dissolved in one quart cold water; let stand until cool.
Melt five pounds grease. Add two tablespoons borax to the lye and
pour the whole slowly into the melted grease, stirring constantly for about
ten minutes. Pour into a pan or mold and score before too hard.

Harvest Muffins

½ cup raisins
¼ cup cold water
1 egg
½ cup cooked pumpkin
½ cup plus 2 tablespoons sugar
½ teaspoon ground allspice
or cloves

½ teaspoon cinnamon
¼ teaspoon salt
3 tablespoons vegetable oil
¾ teaspoon baking powder
¼ teaspoon baking soda
¾ cup plus 2 tablespoons flour

Soak the raisins in the cold water in a bowl for 5 minutes or longer.
Beat the egg in a large mixer bowl. Stir in the pumpkin, sugar, allspice,
cinnamon and salt. Add the oil and mix well. Add the undrained
raisins, baking powder and baking soda and mix well. Add the flour, mixing
gently just until moistened. Fill greased small muffin cups ⅔ full.
Sprinkle with additional sugar if desired. Bake at 400 degrees for 20 to
25 minutes or until the tops spring back when touched. Yields 1 dozen.

Egg Whites

*A pinch of salt added to the white of eggs will make
them beat up quicker and lighter.*

—From *Ye Hingham Cook Book,* 1901

Mother's Daily Bread

2 envelopes dry yeast   2 tablespoons salt
½ cup warm water   5 cups lukewarm water
¼ cup sugar   12 cups flour

Dissolve the yeast in ½ cup warm water. Sprinkle with the sugar
and salt. Combine with 5 cups lukewarm water in a large bowl. Add
the flour and mix well, the mixture will be stiff. Place in a greased bowl,
turning to coat the surface. Let rise, covered, in a warm place for
8 hours or until doubled in bulk. Shape into loaves in 4 loaf pans.
Let rise for 1 hour or until doubled in bulk. Bake at 325 to
350 degrees for 1 hour or until golden brown. You may use this
recipe for rolls if you prefer. Yields 4 loaves.

One Egg

It's hardly enough for breakfast,
It isn't enough when you bake,
It isn't sufficient to make a meringue,
Or bake any cookies or cake.
It doesn't go far in a salad,
Though you devil it, slice it or chop it.
But it covers the floor
From wall to wall
If you drop it.

—From Hingham, Wisconsin

Oat Bread

2 envelopes dry yeast
1 tablespoon sugar
3½ cups warm water
⅓ cup molasses
⅓ cup (scant) sugar

½ cup vegetable oil
1 egg
1 teaspoon salt
6½ cups (or more) flour
1 cup rolled oats

Dissolve the yeast and 1 tablespoon sugar in ½ cup of the warm water in a large bowl. Let stand for several minutes. Add the remaining 3 cups water, molasses, ⅓ cup sugar, oil, egg and salt and mix well. Add the flour and oats and mix well. Place in a greased bowl, turning to coat the surface. Let rise, covered, in a warm place until doubled in bulk. Punch down and let rise again if not ready to knead. Knead on a floured surface until smooth and elastic, adding additional flour as needed. Shape into loaves in 3 large greased loaf pans. Let rise until doubled in bulk. Bake at 350 degrees for 1 hour. Place loaf pans on their sides to cool before removing the bread from the pans. Yields 3 loaves.

Shredded Wheat Bread

4 large shredded wheat biscuits
4 cups boiling water
⅔ cup molasses
6 tablespoons butter
2 teaspoons salt
3 envelopes dry yeast
⅔ cup sugar
1 cup warm water
1 cup wheat germ
10 to 12 cups bread flour
melted butter

Crumble the shredded wheat into a large bowl and add the 4 cups boiling water. Add the molasses, 6 tablespoons butter and salt and mix well. Let stand until lukewarm. Dissolve the yeast and sugar in 1 cup warm water in a bowl. Let stand for several minutes. Add to the wheat mixture and mix well. Stir in the wheat germ. Add the flour gradually, mixing well to form a dough. Place in a greased bowl, turning to coat the surface. Let rise, covered, in a warm place until doubled in bulk. Punch the dough down and shape into loaves in three 5x9-inch loaf pans. Bake at 350 degrees for 1 hour. Brush with melted butter and remove to a wire rack to cool. This recipe may be halved to make 1 large loaf and 1 miniature loaf. Yields 3 loaves.

Overnight Coffee Cake

³/4 cup margarine, softened	1 teaspoon baking soda
1 cup sugar	1 teaspoon nutmeg
2 eggs	½ teaspoon salt
8 ounces sour cream	³/4 cup packed brown sugar
2 cups flour	1 teaspoon cinnamon
1 teaspoon baking powder	½ cup chopped nuts

Cream the margarine and sugar in a mixer bowl until light and fluffy. Beat in the eggs and sour cream. Mix the flour, baking powder, baking soda, nutmeg and salt together. Add to the sour cream mixture and mix well. Spoon into a greased and floured 9x13-inch baking pan. Mix the brown sugar, cinnamon and nuts in a bowl. Sprinkle over the coffee cake batter. Chill, covered, overnight. Bake, uncovered, at 350 degrees for 35 to 40 minutes or until golden brown. Yields 12 servings.

Household Hints
Polish your stove with a piece of Brussels carpet after blacking.
Rub mud stains with a piece of raw potato.

—From *Ye Hingham Cook Book*, 1901

Almond and Nutmeg French Toast

6 (1-inch) slices white or raisin bread

8 eggs, or 4 eggs and egg substitute equivalent to 4 eggs

3 cups milk

¼ cup sugar

½ teaspoon cinnamon

1 tablespoon almond extract

nutmeg to taste

½ cup sliced almonds

Arrange the bread in a buttered 9x13-inch baking dish. Beat the eggs with the milk, sugar, cinnamon and almond extract in a bowl. Pour over the bread. Sprinkle with the nutmeg and almonds. Chill for 4 to 12 hours. Bake at 375 degrees for 45 to 60 minutes or until golden brown. Serve with syrup. Yields 4 to 6 servings.

Queen Anne's Corner

Anne Whiton, born in 1721, was one of seven children and the only one to remain in the family home. Around 1731 she decided to open a public inn on the premises and operated it for almost fifty years. Tradition tells us that Anne was a large muscular woman, known for her impertinence and for speaking her mind boldly and freely to one and all. She came to be called "Quean Anne." Quean in those days meant a disreputable woman. She never married but lived with a man named John Corthell, had three "disreputable" daughters, and kept an "open house." Queen Anne's Corner is on the old stagecoach road between Boston and Plymouth, but the exact location of her tavern is unknown.

Cottage Cheese Yogurt Pancakes

2 eggs
1/3 cup low-fat cottage cheese
3/4 cup nonfat plain yogurt
1/4 teaspoon salt

1/2 cup flour
1/2 teaspoon baking powder
blueberries (optional)

Combine eggs, cottage cheese, yogurt, salt, flour and baking powder in the order listed in a blender container and mix until smooth. Let stand for 10 minutes. Pour a small amount at a time onto a heated griddle. Sprinkle with blueberries. Bake until bubbles in the batter are firm and the bottom is golden brown. Turn the pancakes over and bake until golden brown on the other side. This method of adding the blueberries will keep them from sticking to the griddle. Yields 3 to 4 servings.

Vinegar Hint

A bottle of vinegar and water, half and half, kept by the kitchen sink will be found useful to prevent cracked hands after washing, starching and dish washing.

—From *Ye Hingham Cook Book*, 1901

Favorite Chutney

2 medium-large onions, chopped
8 pears, peeled, chopped
2 apples, peeled, chopped
1½ cups raisins
2 cups vinegar
5½ cups sugar
4 ounces crystallized ginger, chopped

1 (16-ounce) can pineapple tidbits, drained
¼ teaspoon ground ginger
¼ teaspoon ground cloves
¼ teaspoon allspice
¼ teaspoon cinnamon
1 teaspoon crushed red pepper

Combine the onions, pears, apples and raisins in a large stockpot. Add the vinegar, sugar, crystallized ginger, pineapple, ground ginger, cloves, allspice, cinnamon and red pepper and mix well. Simmer for 1 hour or until thickened to the desired consistency. Spoon into hot sterilized half-pint jars, leaving ½ inch headspace; seal with 2-piece lids. Yields 8 half-pints.

Vinegar Hint

Hot cider vinegar will remove paint stains from glass. Remove mildew by soaking in butter milk or putting lemon juice and salt upon it and place in the sun.

—From *Ye Hingham Cook Book,* 1901

Dandelion Jelly

1 quart dandelion blossoms
3 cups water
1 package Sure-Jel

5½ cups sugar
2 teaspoons orange extract

Wash the dandelion blossoms and shake dry. Combine with the water in a saucepan. Bring to a boil and boil for 3 minutes. Drain, pressing the dandelions to remove the liquid; discard the dandelions. Add water if necessary to measure 3 cups liquid. Combine the liquid with the Sure-Jel in the saucepan and mix well. Bring to a boil and add the sugar. Bring to a rolling boil and boil for 3 minutes. Add the orange extract. Skim the mixture and pour into half-pint jars, leaving ¼ inch headspace; seal with paraffin or 2-piece lids. Yields 3 half-pints.

Marmalade

1 grapefruit
3 navel oranges
1 lemon
1 (16-ounce) can crushed
pineapple, drained
grated orange peel (optional)

1 (4-ounce) jar maraschino
cherries, drained, chopped
(optional)
6 cups sugar
½ cup water

Chop the grapefruit, oranges and lemon in a food chopper. Combine with the pineapple, orange peel, cherries, sugar and water in a large stockpot. Simmer for 30 minutes or until the mixture forms a ball when a small amount is dropped into cold water. Spoon into sterilized half-pint jars, leaving ½ inch headspace; seal with 2-piece lids. Yields 8 to 10 half-pints.

102

Old-Fashioned Piccalilli

4 pounds green tomatoes, sliced
medium thick
2 pounds onions, chopped
½ cup salt
4 cups vinegar
1 cup water

1 red bell pepper, chopped
1 pound light brown sugar
1 ounce celery seeds
1 ounce whole cloves
1 ounce mustard seeds
1 ounce whole allspice

Combine the tomatoes and onions in a large bowl. Sprinkle with the salt.
Let stand for 8 hours. Drain, but do not rinse. Combine with the vinegar, water,
bell pepper and brown sugar in a large saucepan. Tie the celery seeds, cloves,
mustard seeds and allspice in a cheesecloth bag. Add to the saucepan. Simmer over
low heat for 2 to 3 hours or until of the desired consistency. Remove the
spices. Spoon into pint jars, leaving ½ inch headspace; seal
with 2-piece lids. Yields 4 to 6 pints.

Freezer Pickles

2 quarts cucumbers
1 onion, sliced
2 teaspoons salt

1½ cups (or less) sugar
½ cup (or more) vinegar

Slice the unpeeled cucumbers very thin. Combine with the onion and
salt in a large bowl. Let stand in a cool place for 2 hours; drain,
but do not rinse. Add the sugar and enough vinegar to cover the slices;
mix well. Spoon into three 1-pint freezer containers. Freeze until
needed. Pickles will stay crisp in the refrigerator after
thawing. Yields 3 pints.

CHAPTER FIVE

Revolutionary Cookies

Cookies ~ Bars

Rainbow Roof House

This most interesting house was built in 1761 by Jabez Wilder at the time of his marriage to Sarah Crocker, and it remained in the Wilder family until 1951. Jabez's great-grandfather, Edward Wilder, came to Hingham in 1637, and was granted a large tract of land south of the Tower Brook. The Rainbow Roof House was built on part of this grant. With its bowed roof and its corners decorated with quoins, or cornerstones, it is considered a well-known landmark in South Hingham.

It is presumed that the bow of the roof resulted when shipbuilders, accustomed to bending timbers to form the hull of a ship, applied this technique to forming the roof of a house. The house is a sophisticated and unique example of the Cape Cod Cottage, one of New England's earliest architectural forms. The style of architecture was first recorded in 1800 by Timothy Dwight, president of Yale, who visited Cape Cod and found "the houses so specialized in character and so closely adhering to a pattern that they ... could be called with propriety, Cape Cod Houses."

Pound Cake Cookies
Ye Hingham Cook Book - 1961

Two cups of white sugar, one cup of butter, two large eggs, one teaspoon of
nutmeg (if preferred lemon extract), three tablespoons milk, one-half teaspoon soda, one
teaspoon of cream of tartar, flour to make soft. After it is mixed put on ice over
night, if you wish to have good luck rolling out; roll very thin.
Cut any shape desired. Sprinkle of sugar before baking.

Refrigerator Molasses Cookies
Sampler of Recipes - 1971

1 cup butter	1/2 teaspoon salt
1 cup brown sugar	3 teaspoons ginger
1 cup molasses	2 1/2 cups flour
1 1/2 teaspoon baking soda	

Put molasses in a saucepan and bring to a boil. Turn off stove and add butter and sugar,
stirring until dissolved. Let cool. Combine and add dry ingredients. Put in greased bread
pan. Store in refrigerator. When hard, slice thinly. Bake 10 minutes 325 to 350.
Watch carefully. I sometimes add grated lemon peel for an extra delicious flavor.
Yields at least 50 cookies.

Spicy Apple Cake Bars

2 cups flour	½ teaspoon salt
1 cup sugar	½ cup margarine, softened
1 cup packed brown sugar	2 large eggs, beaten
2 teaspoons baking powder	2 cups chopped peeled apples
1 teaspoon cinnamon	½ cup chopped nuts
1 teaspoon nutmeg	

Sift the flour, sugar, brown sugar, baking powder, cinnamon, nutmeg and salt into a large mixer bowl. Cut in the margarine until crumbly. Add the eggs and mix well; the batter will be thick. Fold in the apples and nuts. Spread in a greased and floured 9x13-inch baking pan. Bake at 325 degrees for 1 hour. Cool and cut into bars. Yields 2 dozen.

Hingham's Forget-Me-Nots

In the mid-nineteenth century, Hingham artist W. Allan Gay brought home forget-me-not seeds from Fontainebleau in France and planted them along the Town Brook. Not only did the flowers flourish, but they were also a source of income for many enterprising local teenagers, who sold bouquets along the railroad tracks as the trains pulled into the station. Passengers leaned out of the train windows to buy small bunches for ten cents, or larger ones for a quarter. In the early 1900s, when Sunday automobile traffic clogged Hingham Square, boys would jump on the car running boards to make sales. Town Brook became polluted by sewage and industrial waste and was declared a severe health hazard. It was contained underground after World War II, and the forget-me-nots virtually disappeared, but sharp-eyed wildflower enthusiasts can still spot them occasionally in wet and marshy areas.

Apricot Squares

3/4 cup dried apricots
1 cup sifted flour
1/4 cup sugar
1/2 cup butter, softened
1 cup packed brown sugar
1/3 cup flour

1/2 teaspoon baking powder
1/4 teaspoon salt
1/2 teaspoon vanilla extract
1/2 cup chopped pecans or
walnuts
confectioners' sugar

Combine the apricots with water to cover in a saucepan and bring to a boil. Boil for 10 minutes; do not overcook. Drain, cool and chop the apricots; set aside. Sift 1 cup flour and sugar into a bowl. Cut in the butter until crumbly with a pastry blender or fork. Press into a 9x9-inch baking pan. Bake at 325 degrees for 25 minutes. Combine the brown sugar, 1/3 cup flour, baking powder, salt and vanilla in a bowl and mix well. Stir in the pecans and chopped apricots. Spread over the baked layer. Bake for 30 minutes; the top will be soft. Cool and cut into squares. Sprinkle with confectioners' sugar. Yields 9 servings.

Grandmother's Biscotti

3 eggs, beaten
1 cup sugar
½ cup melted margarine
2 teaspoons vanilla extract
1 tablespoon anise extract

1½ cups sliced almonds
2 cups flour
2 teaspoons baking powder
½ teaspoon salt

Combine the eggs, sugar, margarine, vanilla, anise extract and almonds in a mixer bowl and mix well. Sift the flour, baking powder and salt together. Add to the egg mixture and beat until smooth. Add additional flour if needed for an easily handled dough. Divide the dough equally into 2, 3 or 4 portions, depending on the desired size of the biscotti. Shape each portion into a loaf on an ungreased cookie sheet. Bake at 375 degrees for 25 minutes or until brown. Let stand until cool. Reduce the oven temperature to 350 degrees. Cut the cooled loaves into ½-inch slices. Arrange the slices on ungreased cookie sheets. Bake until the biscotti are crisp and golden brown. Let stand until cool. Store in a covered container. Yields 2 dozen.

Carrot Cookies with Orange Frosting

3/4 cup shortening
1 teaspoon salt
1/2 teaspoon vanilla extract
3/4 cup sugar
1 egg

2 cups sifted flour
2 teaspoons baking powder
3/4 cup mashed cooked carrot
Orange Frosting

Cream the shortening, salt and vanilla in a mixer bowl until light. Add the sugar gradually, beating constantly. Add the egg and beat until smooth. Sift the flour and baking powder together. Add to the creamed mixture and mix well. Fold in the mashed carrot. Drop by spoonfuls onto greased cookie sheets. Bake at 350 degrees for 10 to 12 minutes or until golden brown. Remove to wire racks to cool slightly. Frost the warm cookies with Orange Frosting. Yields 40 servings.

~Orange Frosting~

1 tablespoon margarine, softened
1 1/2 tablespoons orange juice
1 tablespoon grated orange peel

1/2 teaspoon almond extract
confectioners' sugar

Beat the margarine, orange juice, orange peel and almond extract in a mixer bowl until smooth. Beat in enough confectioners' sugar to make of the desired spreading consistency.

Frosted Cashew Cookies

2 cups flour
3/4 teaspoon baking powder
3/4 teaspoon baking soda
3/4 teaspoon salt
1/2 cup butter or margarine, softened
1 cup packed brown sugar

1 egg
1/3 cup sour cream
1/2 teaspoon vanilla extract
1 3/4 cups chopped cashews
Browned Butter Frosting
cashew halves

Mix the flour, baking powder, baking soda and salt together. Cream the butter and brown sugar in a mixer bowl until light and fluffy. Beat in the egg, sour cream and vanilla. Add the flour mixture and mix well. Fold in the chopped cashews. Drop by teaspoonfuls onto greased cookie sheets. Bake at 375 degrees for 8 to 10 minutes or until light brown. Cool on a wire rack. Frost the cookies with Browned Butter Frosting. Top each cookie with a cashew half. Yields 2 dozen.

–Browned Butter Frosting–

1/2 cup butter
1 tablespoon cream

1/4 teaspoon vanilla extract
2 cups confectioners' sugar

Melt the butter in a small saucepan and cook until light brown; remove from the heat. Stir in the cream and vanilla. Add the confectioners' sugar and beat until smooth and thick.

Blonde Brownies

2¾ cups flour
2½ teaspoons baking powder
½ teaspoon salt
⅔ cup melted unsalted butter, cooled

1 (1-pound) package light brown sugar
3 eggs
8 ounces chocolate chips
1 cup chopped walnuts

Mix the flour, baking powder and salt together. Combine the butter, brown sugar and eggs in a mixer bowl and blend well. Add the flour mixture and mix well. Stir in the chocolate chips and walnuts. Spread in a buttered 10x15-inch baking pan. Bake at 325 degrees for 35 minutes. Remove the pan to a wire rack to cool slightly. Cut the warm brownies into bars. Yields 3 dozen.

Prize-Winning Recipes

Every August, the Hingham Merchants' Association sponsors SUMMERFEST, when Hingham Square takes on a festive air, with booths, music, children's activities, and a baking contest. Categories include brownies, oatmeal cookies, and chocolate chip cookies. The winners for 1997, chosen by the cookbook committee for the Out of the Ordinary Cookbook are featured on this page and on pages 113, 114 and 123.

 Brownies

4 (1-ounce) squares baking chocolate
½ cup butter
⅛ teaspoon salt
2 cups sugar

2 eggs
1 cup flour
2 tablespoons whipping cream
1 teaspoon vanilla extract
½ cup chopped walnuts

Line an 8x8-inch baking pan with waxed paper. Melt the chocolate and butter with the salt in a double boiler over hot water. Beat in the sugar gradually. Add the eggs 1 at a time, beating well after each addition. Beat in the flour ½ cup at a time. Add the whipping cream 1 tablespoon at a time, beating constantly. Beat in the vanilla. Fold in the walnuts. Pour into the prepared baking pan. Bake at 350 degrees for 39 to 40 minutes. Invert onto a cookie sheet and immediately remove the waxed paper.
Cut into bars. Yields 1⅓ dozen.

Chocolate Chip Cookies

2½ cups flour
1 teaspoon baking soda
½ teaspoon salt
1 cup unsalted butter, softened
¾ cup sugar
¾ cup packed light brown sugar
1 tablespoon vanilla extract

1 tablespoon Frangelico
1 tablespoon Kahlúa
2 large eggs
4 cups milk chocolate chips
1 cup chopped walnuts
1 cup chopped pecans

Mix the flour, baking soda and salt together. Cream the butter, sugar and brown sugar in a mixer bowl until light and fluffy. Add the vanilla, Frangelico and Kahlúa and mix well. Beat in the eggs. Add the flour mixture a few spoonfuls at a time, mixing well after each addition. Stir in the chocolate chips, walnuts and pecans. Drop by rounded tablespoonfuls 2 inches apart onto ungreased cookie sheets. Bake at 325 degrees for 16 minutes or until golden brown. Remove to wire racks to cool. Yields 3½ dozen.

Grandma's Banana Chocolate Chip Cookies

2¼ cups flour
1 teaspoon baking powder
½ teaspoon baking soda
½ teaspoon salt
⅔ cup shortening
1 cup sugar

2 eggs
1 teaspoon vanilla extract
5 tablespoons sour milk
⅔ cup mashed bananas
1 cup chocolate chips

Mix the flour, baking powder, baking soda and salt together. Cream the shortening and sugar in a mixer bowl until light and fluffy. Add the eggs and beat well. Beat in the vanilla. Add the flour mixture alternately with the sour milk and bananas, beating well after each addition. Fold in the chocolate chips. Drop by spoonfuls onto a nonstick cookie sheet. Bake at 400 degrees for 10 minutes or until golden brown. Cool on a wire rack. Yields 2 dozen.

Homesteaders

Many of the present residents of Hingham, Montana, are descendants of the earliest settlers. Ulrich Speiger arrived in Philadelphia from Switzerland in 1737 aboard the ship Charming Nancy. Five generations later, his descendant, Charles Ray Spicher, was born in Pennsylvania and moved to Montana in 1910 to homestead north of Hingham. Charles's great-grandson, William Rodney Spicher, still farms the homestead land. Mildred Sedivy, whose parents were homesteaders in 1910, has lived in Hingham all her life. Rose Kocar has called Hingham her home since 1913.

Chocolate Chip Peanut Butter Bars

4 cups rolled oats
1 cup packed brown sugar
¼ cup corn syrup
⅔ cup margarine, softened

¼ cup chunky peanut butter
1 teaspoon vanilla extract
1 cup chocolate chips
⅔ cup chunky peanut butter

Combine the oats, brown sugar, corn syrup, margarine, ¼ cup peanut butter and vanilla in a large bowl and mix well. Spread in a nonstick 9x13-inch baking pan. Bake at 400 degrees for 12 minutes. Melt the chocolate chips in a double boiler over hot water. Add ⅔ cup peanut butter and mix well. Spread over the baked layer. Cool and cut into bars. Yields 3 dozen.

The Search for Land

In 1847 Leona Cobb and her husband set out to go "somewhere" where government land was available. They took passage on a canal boat from New York and took ten days to make the trip from Troy to Buffalo, because the canal was so crowded with boats that they became lodged together in the locks. After a week's trip from Buffalo to Sheboygan, Wisconsin, they were advised to locate in the vicinity, which they did, buying eighty acres of land for $150 in what would become Hingham, Wisconsin.

Crème de Menthe Squares

½ cup butter or margarine
½ cup baking cocoa
½ cup confectioners' sugar
1 egg, beaten, or equivalent
amount of egg substitute
1 teaspoon vanilla extract
2 cups graham cracker crumbs
½ cup butter or
margarine, softened

⅓ cup crème de menthe or
cream
1½ teaspoons peppermint
flavoring
2 drops of green food coloring
3 to 4 cups confectioners' sugar
¼ cup butter or margarine
1½ cups semisweet chocolate
chips

Heat ½ cup butter and baking cocoa in a saucepan until the butter melts, stirring constantly; remove from the heat. Add ½ cup confectioners' sugar, egg and vanilla and mix well. Stir in the graham cracker crumbs. Pat into an ungreased 10x15-inch pan. Beat ½ cup butter, crème de menthe, peppermint flavoring, food coloring and confectioners' sugar in a mixer bowl until smooth and stiff. Spread over the chocolate layer. Chill in the refrigerator. Melt ¼ cup butter and chocolate chips in a double boiler over hot water. Spread over the mint layer. Chill for 1 to 2 hours. Cut into small squares. Store in the refrigerator. Yields 4 dozen.

Dairy Treasure Bars

1 cup butter
1/2 cup sugar
2 cups flour
1/2 cup cornstarch
4 eggs
4 teaspoons flour
1/2 teaspoon baking powder
2 cups packed brown sugar
1 teaspoon vanilla extract

1/8 teaspoon salt
1 cup shredded coconut
1/2 cup chopped walnuts
1 cup chocolate chips
8 ounces cream cheese, softened
1/2 cup butter, softened
1 teaspoon vanilla extract
4 cups confectioners' sugar

Cream 1 cup butter and sugar in a mixer bowl until light and fluffy. Add a mixture of 2 cups flour and cornstarch and mix well. Press over the bottom of an ungreased 10x15-inch baking pan. Bake at 300 degrees for 25 minutes or until light brown. Beat the eggs lightly in a mixer bowl. Add 4 teaspoons flour, baking powder, brown sugar, 1 teaspoon vanilla and salt and mix well. Stir in the coconut, walnuts and chocolate chips. Spread over the baked layer. Bake for 30 minutes. Let stand until cool. Beat the cream cheese, 1/2 cup butter and 1 teaspoon vanilla in a mixer bowl until smooth. Add the confectioners' sugar gradually, beating constantly. Spread over the cooled baked layers. Cut into bars. Yields 4 dozen.

Jackass Park Gingerbread

1⅔ cups flour   ⅔ cup sugar

1 teaspoon ground ginger 1 egg, lightly beaten

1 teaspoon baking soda ⅔ cup dark molasses

⅔ cup margarine, softened ⅔ cup boiling water

Sift or mix the flour, ginger and baking soda together. Cream the margarine and sugar in a mixer bowl until light and fluffy. Beat in the egg and molasses. Add the flour mixture and mix well. Pour the boiling water into the cup used to measure the molasses; pour into the batter and mix gently. Spoon into a greased 10x10-inch baking pan. Bake at 350 degrees for 40 to 45 minutes or until a wooden pick inserted in the center comes out clean. The gingerbread may fall slightly in the center because it is so soft and light. Serve warm or cold with whipped cream or ice cream. Serve for breakfast by spreading with a little butter and warming briefly in a toaster oven or conventional oven. Do not microwave. Yields 10 to 12 servings.

Jackass Park

There are a number of stories about how this pleasant strip of green got its name.
It was originally a streetcar turnout, used when cars met on the same track.
Later a Hingham resident tied his mules in the area to graze, which may account
for one version. After the car tracks were taken up, the place was unattended,
and some people started a movement to make a park there. As this would involve tearing
out boulders, it was controversial and some complained that it was a "jackass" thing
to do. One day a group of young men went to the area with a soapbox and one of them
made a speech, officially dedicating "Jackass Park." The name has held, despite
occasional efforts to change it to something more genteel.

Rich and Black and Sticky Gingerbread

1½ cups flour

2 teaspoons ginger

2 teaspoons cinnamon

1 cup soft brown sugar

4 ounces (½ cup) golden syrup, corn syrup or maple syrup

½ cup butter

½ cup black treacle or dark molasses

1 cup warm milk

2 teaspoons baking soda

2 eggs, beaten

Grease a deep 7½x11-inch baking pan and line with baking parchment. Sift the flour, ginger and cinnamon together. Combine the brown sugar, golden syrup, butter and treacle in a saucepan. Heat until the butter melts and the mixture is smooth, stirring constantly. Remove from the heat. Stir in the flour mixture. Stir in a mixture of the warm milk and baking soda. Add the eggs and mix well. Pour into the prepared baking pan. Bake at 325 degrees (160 degrees C or Gas 4) for 1 hour or until firm. Remove to a wire rack to cool. Cut into bars. Yields 2 dozen.

Grandma's Hard Ginger Cookies

⅔ cup butter, softened
1 cup sugar
2 eggs, beaten
½ teaspoon baking soda

1 tablespoon (scant) ginger
⅛ teaspoon salt
3½ cups (about) flour
½ to 1 teaspoon sugar

Cream the butter and 1 cup sugar in a mixer bowl until light and fluffy. Add the eggs, baking soda, ginger and salt and mix well. Add enough flour to make a stiff dough. Roll into a rectangle on a lightly floured surface using a ridged rolling pin. Cut into rectangles and sprinkle with ½ to 1 teaspoon sugar. Place on nonstick cookie sheets. Bake at 325 or 350 degrees just until light brown, check after 5 minutes, as cookies will burn easily. Yields 3½ dozen.

West Hingham Hermits

2 eggs
1 (1-pound) package dark brown sugar (2½ cups)
1 cup vegetable oil
3½ cups flour, sifted
1 teaspoon baking soda
2 teaspoons ground cinnamon

½ teaspoon ground ginger
2 teaspoons ground cloves
¼ teaspoon ground nutmeg
⅓ cup milk
2 teaspoons vinegar
1 cup raisins
½ cup chopped walnuts

Beat the eggs, brown sugar and vegetable oil in a mixer bowl until smooth. Add the flour, baking soda, cinnamon, ginger, cloves and nutmeg and mix well. Stir in a mixture of the milk and vinegar. Add the raisins and walnuts and mix well to form a soft dough. Spread on 2 greased 10x15-inch cookie sheets. Bake at 400 degrees for 10 to 12 minutes or just until light brown. Cool slightly and cut into large squares. Yields 6 dozen.

Molasses Cookies

2 cups flour
2 teaspoons baking soda
1 teaspoon cinnamon
½ teaspoon ground cloves
½ teaspoon ground ginger

⅛ teaspoon salt
¾ cup shortening
1 cup sugar
1 egg
⅓ cup molasses

Sift the flour, baking soda, cinnamon, cloves, ginger and salt together.
Cream the shortening and sugar in a mixer bowl until light and fluffy. Beat in
the egg. Add the molasses and the flour mixture and mix well. Chill in the
refrigerator. Shape the dough into 1-inch balls. Place 2 inches apart on a cookie
sheet lined with foil. Bake at 375 degrees for 7 minutes. Remove to
wire racks to cool. Yields 2 dozen.

Oatmeal Coconut Cookies

1 cup shortening
1 cup sugar
1 cup packed brown sugar
2 eggs
2 cups flour
1 teaspoon baking soda

¼ cup boiling water
¼ teaspoon salt
1 teaspoon vanilla extract
3 cups rolled oats
1 cup shredded coconut

Cream the shortening, sugar and brown sugar in a mixer bowl until light
and fluffy. Beat in the eggs. Add the flour and mix well. Dissolve
the baking soda in the boiling water. Add to the flour mixture and mix
well. Beat in the salt and vanilla. Stir in the oats and coconut.
Shape into 1-inch balls. Place 2 inches apart on nonstick cookie sheets.
Bake at 350 degrees for 10 to 12 minutes or until golden brown. You
may also drop the dough by spoonfuls onto the cookie sheets. Yields 4 dozen.

Favorite Oatmeal Cookies

1½ cups flour

1 teaspoon baking soda

½ teaspoon salt

1½ teaspoons cinnamon

1 teaspoon allspice

¼ teaspoon nutmeg

½ cup unsalted butter, softened

½ cup butter-flavor shortening

1 cup packed light brown sugar

1 cup sugar

2 eggs

2 teaspoons vanilla extract

3 cups rolled oats

Mix the flour, baking soda, salt, cinnamon, allspice and nutmeg together. Beat the butter and shortening in a mixer bowl until light and fluffy. Add the brown sugar and sugar and beat well for 2 minutes. Beat in the eggs and vanilla. Stir in the flour mixture. Mix in the oats. Drop by teaspoonfuls onto lightly greased cookie sheets. Bake at 350 degrees for 9 to 10 minutes or until golden brown. Cool on the cookie sheets for 2 minutes. Remove to wire racks to cool completely. Yields 4 dozen.

A Farming Community

In the early days of Hingham, Montana, the town was described as "the progressive city—the city built on a square." Today an attractive park stands in the middle of the square. Hingham is primarily a farming community, although there are some cattle ranches, four grain elevators, and a large fertilizer plant. Farmers mostly raise spring and winter wheat and some barley. The average farm is 2,000 acres—with summer fallow, half of that is planted and harvested each year.

Chocolate-Covered Peanut Bars

1 cup sugar
1/4 cup packed brown sugar
1/2 cup margarine, softened
2 eggs
1/2 teaspoon vanilla extract
1 1/4 cups flour
1 teaspoon baking soda

1 teaspoon salt
1/2 cup (or more) shredded
  coconut
1 (12-ounce) package chocolate-
  covered peanuts
Cream Cheese Frosting

Cream the sugar, brown sugar and margarine in a mixer bowl until light and fluffy. Beat in the eggs and vanilla. Add the flour, baking soda and salt and mix well. Stir in the coconut. Pat into a nonstick 9x13-inch baking pan. Sprinkle with the chocolate-covered peanuts and press down gently. Bake at 350 degrees for 15 to 18 minutes or until golden brown. Cool on a wire rack. Spread with the Cream Cheese Frosting. Cut into bars. Yields 2 dozen.

—Cream Cheese Frosting—

3 ounces cream cheese, softened
1/4 cup margarine, softened
1 tablespoon cream

1/4 teaspoon vanilla extract
1 1/2 cups confectioners' sugar

Beat the cream cheese and margarine in a mixer bowl until smooth. Add the cream and vanilla and mix well. Beat in the confectioners' sugar until smooth.

Pecan Fingers

1 cup butter
½ tablespoon water
1 teaspoon vanilla extract
3 tablespoons confectioners' sugar

2 cups flour
1½ cups finely chopped pecans
confectioners' sugar

Melt the butter in a large saucepan. Add the water, vanilla and 3 tablespoons confectioners' sugar and mix well. Stir in the flour and pecans. Shape into 1½- to 2-inch fingers and place on ungreased cookie sheets. Bake at 200 degrees for 1 hour or until light brown. Roll in additional confectioners' sugar and cool. Store in an airtight container. These cookies freeze well. Yields 2 dozen.

Pecan Delights

2¾ cups packed brown sugar
1 cup butter
1 cup light corn syrup
⅛ teaspoon salt
1 (14-ounce) can sweetened condensed milk

1 teaspoon vanilla extract
1½ pounds pecan halves
1 cup semisweet chocolate chips
1 cup milk chocolate chips
2 tablespoons shortening

Combine the brown sugar, butter, corn syrup and salt in a large saucepan. Cook over medium heat until the sugar is dissolved, stirring constantly. Add the condensed milk gradually, stirring constantly. Cook to 240 to 248 degrees on a candy thermometer, firm-ball stage; remove from the heat. Stir in the vanilla and pecans. Drop by tablespoonfuls onto a waxed-paper-lined cookie sheet. Chill until firm. Melt the chocolate chips with the shortening in the microwave or a double boiler. Drizzle over the clusters. Cool completely. Yields 4 dozen.

CHAPTER SIX

Happy Endings

Cakes ~ Pies ~ Desserts

Old Derby Academy

Although the present structure was not built until 1818, Derby Academy was founded in 1784. The school was the first coeducational institution in New England, and the only source of secondary education in Hingham until 1872. The founder was Madame Sarah Derby, the wealthy widow of Dr. Ezekiel Hersey of Hingham and Captain Richard Derby of Salem.

When the school year opened in 1791, forty male and twenty female students were admitted. Boys and girls were taught separately, however, until 1853. In order to graduate, boys had to make a piece of furniture, and girls were required to complete a sampler. All in attendance had to furnish a share of the firewood.

The original structure is in the Federal style, with large Palladian windows ornamenting the facade. In 1966, the school moved to new quarters, and the old building has been restored, featuring a reception room, ballroom, terrace, and garden. Old Derby Academy now serves as the headquarters for the Hingham Historical Society.

March Meeting Cake

Ye Hingham Cook Book - 1901

In the nineteenth century, before the advent of electricity, town meetings were day-long affairs held in March. By 1872, attendance and interest had increased to such an extent that the Town House was abandoned and a lease was negotiated for the use of Agricultural Hall. Town officers were elected in the morning, after which there was a break for the noon meal. Articles were discussed and voted on during the afternoon. "I was present all day," wrote George Lincoln in 1875, "and enjoyed the proceedings as much as I should a play at the theatre." For those who suffered hunger pangs during these lengthy all-male gatherings, there was the variously called Town Meeting, March Meeting, or 'Lection Cake. The following recipe is for the most experienced and intrepid cooks among us! The "1 cup yeast" called for probably refers to a sourdough starter rather than a cup of yeast as we now know it.

MARCH MEETING CAKE RECIPE

In response to our inquiry for a recipe for March meeting cake a subscriber sends us the following:

Three cups milk, 1 cup yeast, 1 cup sugar, flour enough to make a thick sponge. Make in morning. At night add 1 cup shortening—one-half butter, and one-half lard - 1 cup sugar, salt, 2 cups currants, flour enough to make stiff. Rise over night. In the morning knead and put into pans to rise; then bake.

Hingham Journal, March 20, 1896, page 1

Rhyming Rules for Sponge Cake

Easiest cake to manufacture found in any cookery book.
Just depending on the oven and the deftness of the cook.

Firstly grease the pan with butter—have it ready, near at hand—
Then proceed as follows—strictly to the letter, understand.

Whites and yolks of three eggs parted—drop the whites in larger bowl,
That will be the one remember later to contain the whole.

First the whites beat up together, motion quick, though light of touch.
Then, immediately after beat the yolks, but not too much.

Add to yolks a little lemon, juice or extract, as you please,
Then two teaspoons of cold water, mix together well with these.

To the whites now put the sugar, just a cup, beat these up too,
Add the yolks, continue beating until blending through and through.

Into this a cup of flour stir, as gently as you can,
When you see it turning spongy, quickly pop it in the pan.

And as quickly in the oven which should be a moderate one.
Watch the clock; in twenty minutes usually the cake is done.

Plunge a knitting needle through it—partly opening th' oven door.
Anything adhering to it, you may cook five minutes more.

—From *Ye Hingham Cook Book*, 1901

Almond Butter Cake

2 eggs
3/4 cup sugar
1 teaspoon almond extract
3/4 cup flour

1 teaspoon baking powder
1/2 cup melted margarine or butter
sliced or slivered almonds

Beat the eggs in a mixer bowl until thick and pale yellow. Add the sugar and flavoring. Fold in the flour, baking powder and margarine. Spoon into a greased square cake pan. Sprinkle with additional sugar and almonds. Bake at 350 degrees for 30 minutes. You may double this recipe and bake in 2 layers or in a 9x13-inch pan. Yields 9 to 12 servings.

Fresh Apple Cake

1 1/3 cups vegetable oil
2 cups sugar
2 eggs
3 cups flour
1 teaspoon baking soda
1 teaspoon cinnamon

1 teaspoon salt
2 teaspoons vanilla extract
3 cups chopped peeled Granny Smith apples
1 cup raisins or chopped pecans

Combine the oil, sugar, eggs, flour, baking soda, cinnamon, salt and vanilla in a large bowl and mix well. Stir in the apples and raisins. Spoon into an ungreased 9x13-inch cake pan. Bake at 350 degrees for 1 hour. Substitute other apples for Granny Smith apples or bake in a greased bundt pan for 1 1/4 hours if preferred. Yields 15 servings.

Apricot Brandy Cake

3 cups flour

½ teaspoon salt

¼ teaspoon baking soda

½ cup apricot brandy

1 cup sour cream

½ teaspoon lemon extract

1 teaspoon orange extract or oil

1 cup butter, softened

3 cups sugar

6 eggs

1 teaspoon apricot brandy

Mix the flour, salt and baking soda together. Mix ½ cup brandy, sour cream, lemon extract and orange extract in a small bowl. Cream the butter and sugar in a mixer bowl until light and fluffy. Beat in the eggs 1 at a time. Add the flour mixture and brandy mixture alternately, beating well after each addition. Spoon into a greased and floured large tube pan. Bake at 325 degrees for 1 hour and 20 minutes. Let cool before removing from the pan. Pour 1 teaspoon brandy around the edge of the cake. You may top this with a confectioners' sugar glaze flavored with brandy and orange extract. This cake remains moist for several days. Yields 16 to 20 servings.

Old Derby Ballroom

The ballroom on the second floor of Old Derby Academy was once used for dances, as well as for Hingham town meetings. The space has been elegantly restored as an early eighteenth century ballroom. Nine beautifully draped windows, two fireplaces, fine antique appointments, and portraits set the mood for memorable social evenings, weddings, and other festive occasions.

Chocolate Cake

1 cup flour

1 teaspoon baking powder

½ cup butter, softened

1 cup sugar

4 eggs, at room temperature

1 (16-ounce) can chocolate syrup

1 teaspoon vanilla extract

Mix the flour and baking powder together. Cream the butter and sugar in a mixer bowl until light and fluffy. Beat in the eggs 1 at a time. Add the chocolate syrup and flour mixture alternately, beating well after each addition. Stir in the vanilla. Spoon into a greased and floured 9-inch tube pan. Bake at 350 degrees for 45 to 50 minutes or until a wooden pick inserted near the center comes out clean. Cool in the pan for 10 minutes. Invert onto a cake plate to cool completely. Sprinkle with confectioners' sugar or spread with a favorite frosting. Yields 16 to 20 servings.

Coconut Pound Cake

2 cups flour

1 (7-ounce) package flaked
coconut

2 cups butter, softened

2 cups sugar

6 eggs

1 teaspoon vanilla extract

1 cup sugar

½ cup water

1 teaspoon coconut extract

Mix half the flour with the coconut; set aside. Cream the butter and
2 cups sugar in a mixer bowl until light and fluffy. Add the
remaining 1 cup flour and mix well. Beat in the eggs 1 at a time. Add
the flour mixture and mix well. Stir in the vanilla. Spoon into a
greased and floured 9-inch tube pan. Bake at 350 degrees for 1¼ hours
or until the cake begins to pull away from the side of the pan.
Combine 1 cup sugar, water and coconut extract in a saucepan. Simmer
for 10 minutes. Invert the cake onto a serving plate. Brush the warm
cake with the glaze. Let cool before cutting. You may bake this batter in
six 3x5-inch loaf pans at 325 degrees for 45 minutes. The cake
is better the second day. Yields 16 servings.

Martha's Vineyard Lemon Cake

1½ cups flour

1 teaspoon baking powder

½ teaspoon salt

1 cup sugar

1 cup (scant) butter, softened

2 eggs

½ cup milk

⅓ cup sugar

Juice of 1 large lemon

Grated peel of ½ lemon

Mix the flour, baking powder and salt together. Cream 1 cup sugar and butter in a mixer bowl until light and fluffy. Beat in the eggs 1 at a time. Add the flour mixture and milk alternately, beating well after each addition. Spoon into a greased 5x9-inch loaf pan. Bake at 350 degrees for 45 minutes or until the cake tests done. Heat ⅓ cup sugar, lemon juice and lemon peel in a saucepan until the sugar is dissolved, stirring constantly. Pour over the hot cake. You may bake the batter in 3 smaller loaf pans for 35 minutes. Yields 12 servings.

Her First Attempt

She measured out the butter
With a very solemn air,
The milk and sugar also,
And she took the greatest care
To add the eggs correctly
And a bit of baking powder
Then she stirred it all together
And she baked it full an hour,
But she never quite forgave herself
For leaving out the flour.

—From an old recipe file

Mark Twain's Favorite Sweet Mince Cake

2 cups sifted flour
½ teaspoon salt
½ teaspoon baking powder
½ teaspoon nutmeg
¼ cup brandy
¼ cup whipping cream
1 cup margarine, softened

1 cup sugar
4 eggs
1 (9-ounce) package condensed
  mincemeat, crumbled
2 tablespoons flour
confectioners' sugar (optional)

Sift 2 cups flour, salt, baking powder and nutmeg together. Mix the brandy and whipping cream in a small bowl. Cream the margarine and sugar in a mixer bowl until light and fluffy. Beat in the eggs 1 at a time. Add the flour mixture and brandy mixture alternately, beating well after each addition and beginning and ending with the flour mixture. Combine the mincemeat with 2 tablespoons flour in a small bowl, mixing until the mincemeat is well separated and coated with flour. Fold into the batter. Spoon into a greased and waxed-paper-lined 9- or 10-inch tube pan. Bake at 325 degrees for 1 hour and 20 minutes or until the cake is golden brown and tests done. Cool in the pan for 10 minutes. Invert onto a plate and remove the waxed paper. Sprinkle with confectioners' sugar. Garnish with candied cherries and holly leaves made from green cherries. This cake freezes well. Do not use light margarine in this recipe. Yields 16 servings.

E Plum Cake

1 cup unbleached flour	½ cup margarine, softened
¾ cup sugar	milk or water
1 teaspoon (rounded) cinnamon	1 pound small plums, cut into
⅛ teaspoon salt	halves
2 eggs	

Combine the flour, sugar, cinnamon, salt, eggs and margarine in a
bowl and mix to form a soft dough, adding milk or water if needed. Spread
in an 8-inch sponge cake pan. Arrange the plums cut side up over
the top of the batter. Sprinkle with additional sugar. Bake at 350 degrees
(200 to 240 degrees C) for 30 to 45 minutes or until the
cake tests done. Yields 12 to 16 servings.

The Ties That Bind

The parish church of St. Andrew in Hingham, England, dates from the fourteenth
century and has several ties with Hingham, Massachusetts. Abraham Lincoln's ancestor,
Samuel Lincoln was baptized there in 1622. Apprenticed to a weaver, Lincoln
followed him to America in 1637 to join other settlers from Hingham, England. The bust of
Abraham Lincoln on the north wall of the church was dedicated in 1919 by the
American ambassador, a gift of the people of the United States. The ancient piece of
timber contained in the heavy wooden frame near the south door of the church is
part of one of the beams removed during the restoration of the
Old Ship Church in Hingham, Massachusetts.

Sour Milk Spice Cake

2 cups flour

½ teaspoon baking powder

1 teaspoon (scant) salt

1 teaspoon cinnamon

1 teaspoon (scant) ground cloves

½ teaspoon nutmeg

1 cup sour milk

1 teaspoon baking soda

1½ cups sugar

3 tablespoons shortening

2 eggs

Sift the flour, baking powder, salt, cinnamon, cloves and nutmeg together. Mix the milk and baking soda in a small bowl. Cream the sugar and shortening in a mixer bowl until light and fluffy. Beat in the eggs 1 at a time. Add the flour mixture and milk mixture alternately, beating well after each addition. Spoon into a greased 9x13-inch cake pan. Bake at 350 degrees for 30 to 35 minutes or until the cake tests done. Yields 18 to 24 servings.

Steamed Indian Pudding

One cup of milk, one cup of cream, two cups of Indian meal, one cup of flour, one egg, one teaspoon of sugar and two teaspoons of baking powder. In the absence of cream, milk and a piece of butter about the size of an egg may be substituted as in corn bread. Steam three hours. Serve with sugar or cream or syrup.

This pudding is a favorite with children.

—From *Ye Hingham Cook Book*, 1901

Fairy Cakes

¼ cup margarine or butter, softened
½ cup sugar or superfine sugar
2 eggs
½ cup self-rising flour
1 tablespoon golden (light maple) syrup
1 tablespoon boiling water

Cream the margarine and sugar in a mixer bowl until light and fluffy. Add 1 egg and 2 tablespoons of the flour and beat well. Add the remaining egg and flour and beat well. Spoon the syrup into a small bowl. Add the boiling water with the same spoon and mix well. Add to the batter and beat well. Spoon into paper-lined muffin cups. Place on a baking sheet. Bake at 350 degrees (180 degrees C or Gas mark 4) for 10 to 15 minutes or until the cakes test done. May add golden raisins or flaked almonds to batter. Garnish with quartered glacé cherries or spread with a favorite frosting. These cakes freeze well. Yields 24 cakes.

Fairy Cakes

The recipe for these fairy cakes is from a cook at the Harrow Public School, where Winston Churchill was a student. The boys at the school have always loved them.

Harvest Apple Pie

1 unbaked (9-inch) pie shell
5 cups thinly sliced apples
¾ cup sugar
¼ cup flour
¼ teaspoon salt

½ teaspoon cinnamon
1 cup whipping cream
1 tablespoon sugar
¼ teaspoon cinnamon

Line the pie shell with the apples. Mix ¾ cup sugar, flour, salt,
½ teaspoon cinnamon and whipping cream in a bowl. Spoon
over the apples. Sprinkle with a mixture of 1 tablespoon sugar and
¼ teaspoon cinnamon. Bake at 400 degrees for 50 to 60 minutes
or until the apples are tender and the crust is
golden brown. Yields 8 servings.

Homes

*Over one hundred twenty-five colonial residences and one hundred sixty-five
Federal houses have survived in Hingham. Each June the Hingham Historical Society
sponsors a tour of ten historic Hingham homes and buildings, providing an
opportunity to learn more about the town's enduring past.*

Elegant Apple Apricot Tart

1¼ cups flour
¼ cup sugar
½ cup butter or margarine
2 egg yolks
⅛ teaspoon salt
Grated zest of 1 lemon

5 to 8 Granny Smith or other medium-tart apples, peeled, sliced
1 (12-ounce) jar apricot preserves
2 tablespoons brandy (optional)

Mix the flour and sugar in a bowl. Cut in the butter with 2 forks or a pastry blender until crumbly. Add the egg yolks, salt and lemon zest, mixing until the dough forms a ball. Chill, covered, for 30 minutes or longer. Roll ¾ of the dough into a circle on a lightly floured surface. Fit into a 9-inch pie plate. Fill with the apples, using the largest and most symmetrical for the top layer. Moisten the preserves with the brandy. Spread over the apples, spreading completely to the edge of the pastry. Roll the remaining dough on a lightly floured surface. Cut out with a 3- to 4-inch biscuit cutter, rerolling the dough as needed. Arrange over the apples in a circular pattern, overlapping the edges slightly in a pinwheel pattern. Bake at 425 degrees for 15 minutes. Reduce the heat to 350 degrees. Bake for 30 minutes longer. Yields 8 servings.

Blueberry Pie

1 cup nonfat sour cream

2 tablespoons flour

¼ cup sugar

1 teaspoon vanilla extract

¼ teaspoon salt

1 egg

2½ cups fresh blueberries

1 unbaked pie shell

3 tablespoons flour

1½ tablespoons butter

6 tablespoons chopped pecans

or walnuts

Combine the sour cream, 2 tablespoons flour, sugar, vanilla, salt and egg in a mixer bowl and beat until smooth. Fold in the blueberries. Spoon into the pie shell. Bake at 400 degrees for 25 minutes. Mix 3 tablespoons flour, butter and pecans in a bowl. Sprinkle over the pie. Bake for 10 to 20 minutes longer or until the blueberries are tender and the crust is golden brown. Let stand until cool. Chill until serving time. Yields 8 servings.

No-Bake Blueberry Pie

1 cup blueberries

1 cup sugar

2 tablespoons cornstarch

¾ cup hot water

¼ teaspoon cinnamon

¼ teaspoon salt

3 cups blueberries

juice of ½ lemon

1 baked pie shell

Combine 1 cup blueberries, sugar, cornstarch, hot water, cinnamon and salt in a saucepan. Cook until the mixture thickens and the blueberries are tender, stirring constantly. Stir in 3 cups blueberries gently and remove from the heat. Stir in the lemon juice. Spoon into the pie shell. Chill until serving time. Garnish servings with whipped cream. Yields 8 servings.

Blueberry Tart

½ cup unsalted butter
1 cup flour
2 tablespoons sugar
1 tablespoon white vinegar
1 pint blueberries

2 tablespoons flour
½ to ⅔ cup sugar
1 tablespoon butter
cinnamon

For the pastry, mix ½ cup butter, 1 cup flour and 2 tablespoons sugar in a bowl. Add the vinegar. Shape with floured hands into a ball. Pat into a round 8- or 9-inch tart pan or springform pan; if using a springform pan, pat the dough 1½ inches up the side. Mix the blueberries, 2 tablespoons flour and ½ to ⅔ cup sugar in a bowl. Spread over the dough. Dot with 1 tablespoon butter; sprinkle with cinnamon. Bake at 400 degrees for 40 to 50 minutes or until the blueberries are tender and the crust begins to brown around the edges, stirring once. Let cool for 10 minutes. Remove the side of the pan carefully. May top with additional fresh blueberries. May substitute fresh peaches or plums for the blueberries or mix with the blueberries. Yields 8 to 12 servings.

Cape Cod Cranberry Pie

1½ cups fresh cranberries
½ cup sugar
½ cup chopped walnuts
1 egg

½ cup sugar
½ cup flour
⅓ cup melted butter

Spread the cranberries in a buttered 8-inch pie plate. Sprinkle with ½ cup sugar and walnuts. Beat the egg in a bowl. Add ½ cup sugar and mix well. Add the flour and butter and beat until smooth. Spoon over the cranberries. Bake at 325 degrees for 45 minutes. Serve with vanilla ice cream. Yields 8 servings.

Ruffled Pear Pie

1½ cups flour	⅔ cup sugar
½ teaspoon salt	2 tablespoons cornstarch
1 teaspoon grated orange peel	1 tablespoon butter
½ cup shortening	½ teaspoon salt
3 tablespoons orange juice	1 teaspoon grated orange peel
4 cups chopped peeled Bartlett	3 tablespoons orange juice
pears (about 5 pears)	1 Bartlett pear, sliced

Mix the flour, ½ teaspoon salt and 1 teaspoon orange peel in a bowl.
Cut in the shortening until crumbly. Add 3 tablespoons orange juice, mixing until
the dough forms a ball. Remove and reserve ¼ of the dough. Press the remaining
dough together. Roll into a 12-inch circle on a floured surface. Fit into a
9-inch springform pan, extending dough 1 inch up the side of the pan; flute the
edge of the dough. Combine 4 cups pears, ⅔ cup sugar, cornstarch, butter,
½ teaspoon salt, 1 teaspoon orange peel and 3 tablespoons orange juice in a
saucepan. Bring to a boil, stirring constantly. Simmer for 5 minutes. Spoon
into the pastry-lined pan. Arrange the pear slices decoratively over the top. Roll
the reserved pastry into a 2x14-inch strip; cut into ¾-inch pieces. Twist
the pieces and arrange in a spiral fashion over the pie, moistening the ends
of the dough and pinching together to form a continuous spiral. Bake at
350 degrees for 40 minutes or until light golden brown.
Serve with whipped cream. Yields 8 to 12 servings.

Tun Tavern Pie

¼ cup butter, softened

¾ cup sugar

2 tablespoons flour

1 teaspoon vanilla extract

3 brown eggs

½ cup (or more) Kahlúa

¾ cup evaporated milk

½ cup dark corn syrup

1 cup chopped pecans

1 unbaked (9-inch) pie

shell, chilled

Cream the butter, sugar, flour and vanilla in a mixer bowl until light and fluffy. Beat in the eggs 1 at a time. Stir in the Kahlúa, evaporated milk, corn syrup and pecans. Spoon into the pie shell. Bake at 400 degrees for 10 minutes. Reduce the heat to 330 degrees. Bake for 40 minutes longer or until a knife inserted near the center comes out clean. You may top with whole pecans during the last 10 minutes of baking time if desired. If there is too much filling for the pie shell, use the leftover filling for tarts. Yields 8 servings.

Melville Gardens

In 1871 after several trips to Europe, where he admired the wholesome family atmosphere in German Beer gardens, Samuel Downer opened Melville Gardens, a public day park on forty acres at Crow Point. Many of the visitors were brought by steamboat to Downer's landing to spend the day, and by 1881, a cafe, clambake house, music hall, merry-go-round, mechanical swings, bear pit, monkey cage, various vaudeville attractions, and the Rose Standish Hotel were added. In 1896 the attractions were torn down to build new roads and houses. Nothing remains of Melville Gardens today, but some people say that if you listen closely on a summer day, you can hear the musical strains from Edmand's Band that once played there.

Arthur's Favorite Bread Pudding

Hingham author Marc Brown, author of the children's book series about Arthur the Aardvark, now an animated PBS program, contributes this rich and delicious bread pudding recipe, adapted from *The Oyster Bar Cookbook*.

French bread	2 eggs
2 cups whipping cream	2 egg yolks
1 cup light cream	2 teaspoons vanilla extract
3/4 cup sugar	1 tablespoon orange liqueur
2 ounces bittersweet chocolate	1 teaspoon instant coffee powder
2 ounces unsweetened chocolate	1 teaspoon hot water
1/8 teaspoon salt	2 cups whipped cream

Trim the crust from the bread; cut enough of the bread into 2-inch cubes to measure 2 cups. Reserve the remaining bread for another use. Place the bread cubes in a 9x9-inch baking pan or baking dish. Combine the whipping cream, light cream, sugar, bittersweet chocolate, unsweetened chocolate and salt in a heavy saucepan. Bring to a simmer. Cook over medium heat until the chocolate melts, stirring constantly. Beat the eggs and egg yolks in a bowl. Stir a small amount of the hot mixture into the eggs; stir the eggs into the hot mixture. Add the vanilla and liqueur. Pour over the bread cubes. Let stand for 20 minutes, tossing frequently to moisten the bread. Set the baking pan in a larger pan of hot water. Bake at 325 degrees for 15 minutes. Stir well. Bake for 10 minutes longer or just until set; the center should still be soft. Cool slightly. Combine the coffee powder and hot water in a cup, stirring until the coffee powder is dissolved. Fold into the whipped cream. To serve, spoon warm pudding into warm bowls and top with the coffee-flavored whipped cream. Yields 8 to 10 servings.

Marc Brown

Hingham Pudding

2½ cups flour	¾ cup molasses
¼ cup sugar	¾ cup milk
1 teaspoon baking powder	½ cup melted butter or
1 teaspoon cinnamon	margarine
½ teaspoon baking soda	½ cup chopped pecans
¼ teaspoon ground cloves	Poached Apples and Pears
2 eggs, beaten	Sherried Custard Sauce

Mix the flour, sugar, baking powder, cinnamon, baking soda and cloves
in a large bowl. Mix the eggs, molasses, milk and butter in a medium bowl. Stir
into the flour mixture. Fold in the pecans. Spoon into a greased and floured
8-cup fluted tube pan. Cover the pan with foil, securing with kitchen string if
needed. Place the pan on a rack in a deep kettle. Add enough boiling water to the
kettle to reach 1 inch up the tube pan. Steam, covered, for 1½ hours or until a
wooden pick inserted near the center comes out clean, adding water to the kettle
if needed. Let stand for 10 minutes. Unmold carefully. Let stand on a wire rack
for 30 to 40 minutes or until slightly cool. To serve, place the pudding on a
shallow plate. Arrange Poached Apples and Pears around the pudding.
Pour the syrup from the fruit around the pudding. Serve with
Sherried Custard Sauce. Yields 12 servings.

*This pudding recipe has been updated for modern cooks. It can be
served alone or with Poached Apples and Pears
and Sherried Custard Sauce recipes, which are included here.*

—Poached Apples and Pears—

1 cup water
1/2 cup sugar
2 teaspoons lemon juice
2 large apples, cored, cut into
6 wedges

3 large pears, cored, cut into
6 wedges
3 tablespoons orange liqueur

Bring the water, sugar and lemon juice to a boil in a 12-inch skillet. Add the apples and pears. Simmer, covered, for 10 to 12 minutes or just until the fruit is tender, turning occasionally. Remove the fruit to a bowl with a slotted spoon. Boil the syrup in the skillet for 4 minutes or until reduced to 1/3 cup. Stir in the liqueur. Yields 12 servings.

—Sherried Custard Sauce—

2 egg yolks, beaten
2 tablespoons sugar
1/8 teaspoon salt

3/4 cup milk
1 tablespoon cream sherry
1/2 teaspoon vanilla extract

Combine the egg yolks, sugar, salt and milk in a small heavy saucepan. Cook over medium heat until the mixture begins to thicken and coats a metal spoon, stirring constantly. Remove from the heat. Pour into a bowl set in a larger bowl of ice water. Stir the sauce constantly for 1 to 2 minutes or until slightly cool. Stir in the sherry and vanilla. Chill, covered, until serving time. Yields 1 cup.

Dessert Cream with Raspberry Sauce

1 tablespoon unflavored gelatin
½ cup milk
1 cup light cream
¾ cup sugar

1 cup sour cream
1 teaspoon vanilla extract
Raspberry Sauce

Sprinkle the gelatin over the milk in a saucepan. Let stand until softened. Add the cream and sugar. Heat over low heat until the gelatin and sugar are dissolved, stirring constantly. Cool slightly. Fold in the sour cream and vanilla, stirring gently until most of the lumps are gone. Spoon into a mold. Chill until firm. Serve with Raspberry Sauce. Yields 6 servings.

~Raspberry Sauce~

1 (10-ounce) package frozen raspberries
½ cup red currant jelly

1 tablespoon cornstarch
1 tablespoon butter
¼ cup orange juice

Combine ¾ cup of the raspberries with the jelly in a saucepan. Bring to a simmer. Stir the cornstarch into the remaining raspberries. Add to the mixture in the saucepan. Cook until thickened, stirring frequently. Cook for 2 minutes longer, stirring constantly. Remove from the heat. Add the butter. Let cool. Add the orange juice. Chill until serving time. Yields 1½ cups.

Chocolate Soufflé

½ cup baking cocoa	¼ teaspoon salt
1 cup milk	3 egg yolks
2 tablespoons butter	1 teaspoon vanilla extract
3 tablespoons flour	3 egg whites, stiffly beaten
½ cup sugar	

Beat the cocoa and milk in a bowl with a rotary beater until smooth, set aside. Melt the butter in a saucepan. Stir in the flour, sugar and salt. Add the milk mixture. Bring to a boil, stirring frequently. Let cool. Stir in the egg yolks and vanilla. Fold in the egg whites. Spoon into a buttered baking dish. Set the baking dish in a pan of water that is larger than the baking dish. Bake at 350 degrees for 40 to 45 minutes or until set. Serve with whipped cream. Yields 6 servings.

Daniel Webster

Orator and statesman Daniel Webster was known to leave his Boston law office and head for Hingham by boat. There his coachman would meet him and drive him to his farm in Marshfield, but not before he stopped at the Old Ordinary for refreshment. He was apparently very fond of the mulled wine punch prepared by the proprietor's wife, Mrs. Wilder. Webster's traveling desk is on display at the Old Ordinary.

Heavenly Lemon Torte

1 package graham crackers, crushed
¼ cup melted butter
6 egg whites
¾ teaspoon cream of tartar
¼ teaspoon salt
1¼ cups sugar

2 tablespoons cornstarch
¾ cup sugar
1 cup water
6 egg yolks, beaten
juice of 1 lemon
1 cup whipping cream, whipped

Press a mixture of the graham cracker crumbs and butter into a 9x13-inch baking pan. Beat the egg whites, cream of tartar and salt in a mixer bowl until soft peaks form. Add 1¼ cups sugar gradually, beating constantly until stiff peaks form. Spread over the crust. Bake at 250 degrees for 1 hour. Combine cornstarch, ¾ cup sugar and water in a saucepan. Add the egg yolks and lemon juice. Cook until thickened, stirring frequently. Cool slightly. Spread over the meringue layer. Let cool. Top with the whipped cream. Chill, covered, for several hours or overnight. Yields 15 servings.

Truffle Torte

ground nut oil

75 grams (3 ounces) amaretti
cookies, finely crushed

450 grams (1 pound) plain
dessert chocolate or luxury
cooking chocolate, broken
into pieces

5 tablespoons corn syrup

5 tablespoons rum

570 grams (1 pint) whipping
cream, at room temperature

sifted baking cocoa

2 tablespoons amaretto (optional)

light cream

Brush the bottom and side of a 9-inch springform pan lightly with ground nut oil. Line the pan with waxed paper. Sprinkle the cookie crumbs in the pan. Combine the chocolate, corn syrup and rum in a heatproof bowl. Set the bowl over a saucepan of barely simmering water. Heat until the chocolate has melted, stirring until smooth. Remove from the heat. Let stand for 5 minutes or just until lukewarm. Beat the whipping cream in a mixer bowl until slightly thickened. Fold half the whipped cream into the chocolate mixture, then fold the chocolate mixture into the remaining whipped cream. Spoon into the prepared pan. Chill, covered with plastic wrap, overnight. Place on a serving plate and remove the side of the springform pan. Dust with baking cocoa. Mark the top of the torte into serving sections if desired. Stir the amaretto into light cream. Serve with the torte. Yields 8 to 12 servings.

CHAPTER SEVEN

Et Cetera

Contributors — Index

Hingham Harbor

Since its earliest days, Hingham harbor has been an important part of the town's economy, providing the source of food and employment to Hingham residents. Following the Revolution, Hingham realized the economic potential of its coastal location. Several large fishing fleets brought in hake, cod, and mackerel, and shipbuilding became an important industry, as did a thriving rope walk.

The nineteenth century saw many steamboats carrying passengers and freight between Hingham and Boston, and this tradition continues today as daily commuter boats provide convenient and pleasant service to Boston and Logan Airport. During World War II, the harbor and town were dramatically changed by the building of an extensive shipyard at Huet's Cove. LSTs (Landing Ship Tanks) were constructed there as well as destroyer escort vessels for both the British and the U.S. navies.

Today the harbor is home to many recreational boats. It is also the site of a charming bandstand, where summer concerts are featured, and Hingham families enjoy firework displays on the Fourth of July.

Contributors

The enthusiastic response to our request for recipes was gratifying, and we only wish that we had been able to use every single one. Unfortunately, space limitations prevented us from including recipes from every contributor, but cooks in every Hingham around the world can be proud of their roles in continuing their own towns' culinary tradition.

Pamela Achille
S. V. Arnold
Beryl Baker
Harriet Baker
Sandra Baker
Carol Jones Balch
Brenda Berres
Inga Bisbee
Geneva Tower Blaine
Ann Thorne Blanchard
Lynn Bonanno
Joan Bouve-Ramsay
Bowl and Board
Hazel Brekke
Clementine Brown
Marc Brown
Shirley Brown
Harriet W. Buckley
M. Bunch
Carol Cavanaugh
Helen Chamberlain
Jan Colby
Betty Cole
Betsy Cornwall
Sheila Crehan

Helen Cronin
Gladys L. Cushing
Iris Daigle
Deborah Danforth
Jean Hoss De Forest
Deb Deruyter
Margo Dickinson
Judi Ditsworth
Laura Dolfin
Muriel L. Douglass
Geri Duff
Mary Duff
Bev Dulmes
Carol Dulmes
Denise Faith Dulmes
Laura L. Dulmes
Beverly Dykstra
Edie Earle
Susie Belding Eldredge
Fran Endicott
Theana Evangelides
Vicki Fitzgerald
Pat Fogarty
Beverly Garside
Roberta C. Gilbert

Helen Grady
Eileen Gray
Joy Greedy
Tony Greedy
Beverly Groseclose
Annette Gryglewski
Stephanie Haff
Edith Key Haines
Winston Hall
Ernest Hancock
Christine Hanses
Cindy Harmeling
Lorena Laing Hart
Francis Russell Hart
Ellen Harvey
Sharon Hawkins
Bill Hentzl
Nancy Herstad
Hingham Society,
Hingham, England
Joan Hintz
Janice L. Hirsch
Delores Hoitink
Clara Hoopman
Priscilla Hoxie

Janna Huenink
Dave Jackson
Norma Jackson
Moira Jewsbury
Hazel Jochim
Diane Jumper
Mildred Kaat
Elizabeth Kannberg
Donna Kearney
Rose Kocar
Roberta Krause
Joyce Kuhlow
Jean Kurtz
Eunice R. Lammers
Jennifer Land
Mary L. Longo
Louise Luther
Judy Lyons
Louise M. Mable
Arline MacKay
Liz Mackay
Brian Mackey
Christine Mackey
Ruth MacLean
Amelia Mangold
Kym Marcella
Judy Margetts
Judith Mehring
Ruth Mentink
Jo Ann Mitchell
Dorothy D. Monroe
Ginny Moore

Audrey Muir
Cathy Mulvaney
Mary Jo Murphy
Priscilla Wadleigh Murray
Lily Mae Myers
Virginia Nelson
Mary Niles
Bette Owens
Dorothy Palmer
Linda Patrick
Elisabeth Patterson
Katie Pelletier
Cheryl A. Peterson
Joan Philipon
Betty Potter
Nat Preston
Jane Pritchard
Ellen D. Prusick
Betty Pyne
Kathy Raunig
Mildred Rauwerdink
Ken Read-Brown
Ann Reardon
M. Reid
Adrienne Richardson
Jean Roche
Phyllis Rodgers
Valerie Rogers
Jane M. Runo
Joyce Gray Schreier
Audrey Semmence
Mildred Sedivy

Carol Siegl
Audrey Snuske
Sharon Spicher
Jeanette Stebbins
Geraldine de R. Stein
William Stenzl
Pauline Stickland
Jackie Stoffregen
Marilyn Stokdyk
Avis Studley
Barbara Sullivan
Carol Sullivan
Karen Ten Haken
Mary Lynn Ten Haken
Jack Thomas
Janet Thompson
Michael E. Thompson
A. Putnam Tower
Rose Tuite
Barbara Veldboom
Louise Villett
Edward T. Wadleigh
Dorothy R. Wagstaff
Maureen Watson
Rita Watson
Adeline Webster
Peggy Weymouth
Cynthia Wilkins
Vera Williams
Andrea Wilson
Faye Zimmer
Annette Zipfel

Index

157

Out of the Ordinary®

Hingham Historical Society
P.O. Box 434
Hingham, Massachusetts 02043

Please send ____ copies of *Out of the Ordinary* at $16.95 each $ _____

Plus postage and handling at $3.20 each $ _____

Massachusetts residents add sales tax of $ .85 each $ _____

Total $ _____

Name _____

Address _____

City _____   State _____   Zip _____

Make checks payable to: Hingham Historical Society

Out of the Ordinary®

Hingham Historical Society
P.O. Box 434
Hingham, Massachusetts 02043

Please send ____ copies of *Out of the Ordinary* at $16.95 each $ _____

Plus postage and handling at $3.20 each $ _____

Massachusetts residents add sales tax of $ .85 each $ _____

Total $ _____

Name _____

Address _____

City _____   State _____   Zip _____

Make checks payable to: Hingham Historical Society

ballerina possessing a strong individuality and exuberant enthusiasm for her vocation. One never wishes for another dancer when watching her in a rôle.

Her performance as Zarema in *The Fountain of Bakhchisarai* is charged with meaning and she expresses to perfection both her joy at the return of the Khan Girei and her uncontrollable jealousy of her new rival Maria.

M. Gotlieb

A ballerina with great charm and flawless execution in *demi-caractère* rôles but yet to develop fully from the histrionic point of view, she is definitely one of the most pleasing and polished dancers in the company.

Like Struchkova, she possesses a flawless technique which allows her to perform the most difficult solos with complete absence of visible strain or effort.

The rôle of Jeanne in *Flames of Paris* suits her to perfection but in purely classical rôles such as the Diamond Fairy in *The Sleeping Beauty* she fails to give the sparkle which her technical excellence should allow her to convey to the full.

As Pascuala in *Laurencia* she has a rôle suiting perfectly her gay personality and she executes all her solos and *pas de deux* with brilliance. She still has to develop more feeling in the more dramatic scenes with Laurencia. She is also excellent in the *pas de trois* with Laurencia and Jacinta and in the *pas de six* with Lepechinskaya and Bogolubskaya when partnered by Andrianov, Kondratov and Evdokimov.

Y. D. Sekh

An outstanding, elegant dancer with dramatic talent and an accomplished tecnique, exceptional light elevation and forceful personality.

As Mercutio in *Romeo and Juliet* he gives a fine performance in the death scene (Act II, Scene 3).

G. Evdokimov

A very strong classical and character dancer, his rôles vary from purely classical to the savage Nur Ali in *The Fountain of Bakhchisarai*.

He possesses extraordinary virility and musicality. As Nur Ali he gives more colour, excitement and vigorous abandon to this one part than most companies in the West manage to create with their full *corps de ballet* and soloists. His sensitive, expressive miming is of the highest order and while one may first of all think of him in full blooded character rôles, in classical work he has a noble appearance and faultless technique, making him one of the most valuable soloists at the Bolshoi today.

P. M. Andrianov

A young dancer of perfect classical technique and natural noble appearance he stands out in *ensemble* work. His fencing variation in *The Fountain of Bakhchisarai* (Act I) is of such excellence and lightness that this act loses much when he is absent from the rôle.
With Evdokimov in *Laurencia* he is outstanding.

Yuri Zhdanov

Another excellent technician and lyrical soloist, he is a good partner if sometimes limited dramatically.
In *The Fountain of Bakhchisarai* as Vatslov he is ideally cast and dances his variations to perfection, demonstrating his unusual elevation. In *Romeo and Juliet* he sometimes fails to maintain the character of the rôle throughout but in the tender and romantic scenes with Juliet he is the true Romeo, while in the scene of Juliet's funeral he gives a very moving performance accomplishing the difficult choreography without apparent effort. He is also excellent as Albrecht in *Giselle*.

N. Chistova

We shall know much more of Chistova not so very long from now. She is a dancer brimming over with poetic romanticism with every movement of her expressive limbs.
She possesses a beautiful long line and, like most of the other young soloists in the company, he is technically remarkably strong.
Having the necessary romantic appearance and expression, she gives a convincing performance as Parasha in *The Bronze Horseman*. Her solo work is a delight to watch and in *pas de deux* her line is tender and lyrical while her acting ability is strongly developed.
As Princess Florina in *The Sleeping Beauty* she gives a polished performance in the Bluebird *pas de deux*. But, while her *variation* is technically perfect, her interpretation is rather more romantic than we are accustomed to in the West.
However, the choreography of most of the *variations* in this ballet differs greatly from the versions generally presented by companies outside the U.S.S.R. and if one misses sparkle in the Bolshoi *variations* it is due to the new choreographers and not the dancers.

M. Bogolubskaya

A sensitive artist with an exceptionally wide range, her fragile appearance is in contrast to her very positive and expressive movements on stage.
As Jacinta in *Laurencia* she gives an emotionally complete rendering of the ravished girl and maintains her character throughout, accomplishing all the difficult choreography with ease and fluent grace. In the second act she proves herself an exceptional actress as well as a musical and lyrical dancer.